The Sun Stood Still

Books by Roderick MacLeish

Roderick MacLeish

THE SUN STOOD STILL

Atheneum   New York

1967

APR 4 1969

To Bernard Redmont

the Paris correspondent of the Westinghouse
Broadcasting Company, whose courage and
compassion in reporting from Cairo during
the days that the sun stood still deepened the
affection and respect that his colleagues and
friends bear him

. . . Then spoke Joshua to the Lord in the day when the Lord delivered up the Amorites before the children of Israel, and he said in the sight of Israel, Sun, stand thou still upon Gideon; and thou, moon, in the valley of Aij'alon. And the sun stood still, and the moon stayed, until the people had avenged themselves upon their enemies. . . .

THE BOOK OF JOSHUA

Preface

OF ALL FORMS OF TRAGEDY, war is the least intimate. It is, as Clausewitz says in his gloomy aphorism, an extension of politics by other means; that is, war is the surrender of a reasonable process to an unreasonable one. In the abstract, war retains the objectives of politics —security, acquisition, deterrence and the imposition of the national will. Specifically, it raises the problem of murder to a level of such magnitude that murder ceases to be a problem and becomes an achievement.

All of this is perfectly obvious when war is considered with detachment. To those who witness actual wars and manage to overcome the exhilaration of being on the winning side or the despair of watching the losers lose, these truisms take on a vivid sort of reality.

Toward the end of May 1967 my editors suggested that I might want to travel out to Cairo for a week and then to Tel Aviv for another week to write and broadcast some commentaries on the general situation in the Middle East. Some of our staff correspondents in Europe had already arrived in each capital; the idea was that analysis might be a useful supplement to their daily news reports. I agreed to the proposal. I had traveled through a good bit of the Arab world, but I had never been to Israel. I flew to London on May 26—it was my home for many years—visited with friends and went on to Cairo on May 28. I stayed there until Friday, flew to Rome for the week end and proceeded to Tel Aviv on the following Sunday, June 4. The war broke out on Monday, June 5. Obviously, the nature of events had changed my assignment: I became a reporter again instead of a commentator. It was not the first war I had seen. But it was the first classic one. There were two armies (if one can call the combined Arab forces a single army) and set battlefields. Those who were killed were, for the most part, soldiers and not civilians. This war had a beginning and a conclusive end—unlike most of the recent wars in history, starting with Korea.

Following armies and writing about their activities is an intense and isolating experience. One sees events that are—in the exact meaning of the word—extraordinary. A human body lying beside a smashed-up automobile on a highway shocks. The litter of death that is part of an advancing army's refuse ceases to shock after the observer has passed through the first shoal of corpses; different and degrading reactions set in. A wrecked train in Iowa is a naked bit of carnage in an orderly landscape; what is left of an ammunition train that has been rocketed by a Mirage III is just another bit of a grand design that is becoming evident to the advancing observer. Thus, the extraordinary becomes ordinary until one returns to the usual order of the familiar world. It is only then that shocked contemplation begins.

At the same time, the observer is cut off from all the mass of extenuation that flows like a tide toward and away from the actual war. Politics and diplomacy don't cease when nations decide to extend them by other means; they just continue in irrelevant futility. Far away from the actual war, opinions are being formed, speeches are being made and decisions are being taken. The one who is witnessing the war only finds out about this later. To many of the men and women who, as journalists, observed the third Arab-Israeli war, some of the opinions that were formed during it came as a shock; there was a tendency among many Western newspapers and commentators to treat the war as either a triumph of simple good over simple evil or as a sort of huge Jewish joke. Some of the speeches that were made during the eight days of the war were grotesque—one has in mind the Soviet ambassador to the United Nations. And some of the decisions that were taken had the true quality of the absurd in that they were not based on any real knowledge of the war that was then in progress.

At the same time, one finds that the conflict which has commanded one's whole attention was, to many people off in the distance, nothing more than a device to carry on other arguments. Almost before the first day of the third Arab-Israeli war was over, its meaning was being drawn into the great American debate over Vietnam. The historian Barbara Tuchman had written a letter to *The New York Times* suggesting that there were differences between the two wars—differences of magnitude, motive and morality. She was immediately attacked and called ambivalent. But she was right. War carries no uniform definition; when you have seen one of them, you have not seen them all. Only the soldiers are the same. But soldiers do not start wars. Politicians, generals and statesmen caught in the determinations of history are the authors of war.

All of these arguments, opinions, speeches and decisions are, however, taking place beyond the scene of the war. The witnesses who are in the belligerent capitals or upon the battlefields have abandoned for the moment everything they know about the causes and have become absorbed in the process of the war itself. It is, for them, an experience isolated in the sensibilities by its shocking and extraordinary nature. Only later do the witnesses integrate the war itself into what they know about its causes. Then, because the event was such a crucial experience, the witnesses come to the conclusion that what they know of the causes is not sufficient to explain the violence they have seen. They seek further in the history and the psychology of both sides. As more explanations for what has happened suggest themselves, the original partisanship of the witness for one side or the other grows weaker. He comes first to the conclusion that the decisive question is not who started the war but who caused it. Then he discovers that the cause was not simple. It may have been in preparation for ten years or a thousand years. He abandons the idea of a single villain—except in cases such as Adolf Hitler or Joseph Stalin—and discovers that fallibility in running the affairs of a belligerent country may explain more than villainy, in analyzing the cause of the war. He begins to think about other wars from Kossovo to the Crimea, from World War I to Vietnam, and he concludes that there is no single or universal cause for them. War is as complex in its origins as love. The witness abandons his search among archives and graveyards for a simple explanation; he settles for an infinite number of causes and returns, at last, to the particular war that preoccupies him. If he has begun to understand the essential nature of war's public tragedy—its accidental aspects, its debt to a failure of human understanding, its abandonment of the reasonable process of politics for the unreasonable science of murder—then he has gained something useful from his participation in the extraordinary.

As one singularly unequipped to make moral judgments on the behavior of people or countries, I have not written this essay as a tract that tries to justify anyone or anything. I am not an historian, nor am I a qualified student of military tactics. The ultimate history of the third Arab-Israeli war will be many years in preparation and the final analysis of its science awaits the attention of a literate general or some other improbable figure.

In the final analysis, it should not be a journalist's task to simplify complicated events. He should try as hard as he can to include the complexities. There is always the risk that he will be accused of blurring matters so that the crystal clarity of virtue and the black silhouette of fault become confused in the machinery of circumstance.

But that can't be helped.

Acknowledgments

A GOOD MANY PEOPLE have contributed in all sorts of ways to the writing of this book. Colleagues in journalism from Europe, Great Britain, the United States and Israel gave freely of their notes, memories, theories, printed and broadcast material with no thought of compensation or competition. Friends in the diplomatic corps of France, the United Kingdom, the United States, Turkey, Iran, Israel, the United Arab Republic and the Hashemite Kingdom of Jordan who expressed themselves with such candor must, obviously, remain anonymous. My gratitude to all of them is very great indeed.

The planning and writing of the book would simply not have been possible without the work of my friend and colleague Ruth Daniloff, who took on a heavy research and critical task and executed it brilliantly. My wife and children listened patiently to bits of the manuscript being read as it was written and, in the midst of remodeling a new house, managed to produce the atmosphere that was indispensable to the writing. To them, also, my great thanks.

One special friend in London was responsible for the thought that led to the book itself. Simon Michael Bessie of Atheneum Publishers in New York helped to talk it into life.

All of these people contributed many of the mosaic pieces that went into the final manuscript. So did the Israeli guide officers in the Sinai, the police of Natanya, the cadres of the Arab Socialist Union in Cairo and those others, official and unofficial, whose words and acts are parts of the final impression. To contribute to the whole is not to bear responsibility for it. All of these people did their best to help, and if the end result is flawed, it is because I did not understand them properly or failed to utilize their help in the best way.

I am also grateful to the news department and executives of the Westinghouse Broadcasting Company for their donation of research facilities, their permission to use broadcast scripts and, above all, for easing the time pressures to enable me to write.

Contents

CAIRO

May 28-June 2

Here I am, an old man in a dry month,
Being read to by a boy, waiting for rain.

T. S. ELIOT

IF THE ARMIES OF EGYPT WERE AS AGGRESSIVE AS the flies of Cairo, the Arabs would conquer the world again. The flies are a final indignity in Egypt. They swarm on the faces of living children and appear by millions in the unnourishing desert to devour the dying and the dead. The flies and an exhausting liver disease make Arab flesh miserable while the Arab soul dreams of a brilliant past and a perfect paradise to come; there will be cool rivers and lavish gardens and presumably no flies when life ends for the virtuous.

The God of Islam obviously loves the Arabs because he chose their language to reveal himself in his final form to one of them. But God didn't presume to make life easy for his children. Nor did he make it beautiful. The deep blue of the Mediterranean is the last full color that the traveler sees when he flies from Europe to Egypt. Thereafter the eye dwells in a mixture of dull monochromes. The Nile delta is grayish green where plants grow under an infinite powdering of dust from the desert. Villages lie like scabs of dead tissue upon the earth.

When British Overseas Airways Corporation's Flight 208 from London landed at Cairo on the third Sunday of May, it was 6:15 in the evening. The sun hung like a burning brass ball in the sky over the western desert, yet its light had the ubiquitous brilliance of noon. In northern hemispheres the sun is in endless contest with the earth's green, snow and gold. In the Middle East the sun won its struggle with the ground epochs ago.

There were only twenty passengers on the London flight and most of them were going to India or the Far East. Travel to, even through, Cairo wasn't popular at that point. The British week-end press was full of the Middle Eastern crisis; Egyptian troops were lined up in the Sinai opposite the Israelis, Jordan was mobilizing and Syrian artillery boomed at northern kibbutzim from the Heights of Golan. The tyrannic hatred that the Arabs, Israel and the rest of the world had accepted as normal had suddenly gone critical, diverting attention away from the carnal monotony of Vietnam. On Friday the *Economist* had said, "If this isn't the way a third world war happens, it's a pretty good imitation."

Yet there were none of the usual signs of girding for war as the BOAC aircraft circled east, south and then descended on a northward path to land at Cairo. Transport planes sat in the sun on the concrete paths of a fighter base. There were no MIG's in sight. There were no anti-aircraft guns. Sparse traffic moved on the roads, and the only sudden movement was the flash of sun on a car's windshield.

Only two passengers got off at Cairo. Heat wrapped them and the flies clustered as the bus went in to the terminal building set on a sandy knoll. Egyptian airport staff in smart uniforms joked with the British stewardesses. In the dark landing hall, customs men, immigration officials and porters were standing in front of a television set listening to President Nasser give a press conference. The few who had detached themselves to attend to the passengers were almost pointedly polite to an arriving American. "America," President Nasser was saying in Arabic, "is creating a great commotion in the world. America, which created Israel and which protects Israel, now attempts to complicate and exaggerate matters."

He was rotating before the world. The separate and sometimes contradictory planes of his nature were throwing out flashes of revelation to his listeners. Nasser was readjusting history that afternoon. Egypt, he said, was getting rid of the effects of the aggression that Israel had committed during the Suez war of 1956. Israel's victory in the Sinai-Suez affair had been false and the Israelis were deceived by it. This was the semantic Nasser, the brilliant orator in two sorts of Arabic, whose splendid self-confidence was a palliative to the historic aggrievement of his people.

A Lebanese correspondent had suggested that the Arabs blow up their oil wells to "cut the veins" of America in the Middle East. That part of Nasser which can erect logic in the middle of the emotional flow from oratory rejected the idea. "These," he said of the oil wells, "are our interests, our wealth and not the Americans'."

And the Nasser who can often translate his charisma into useful acts of diplomacy seemed to sense that if the crisis were to end in negotiation General de Gaulle was the only possible intermediary. He praised France for a lack of bias, while damning the United States, Britain and West Germany as the weapons merchants for Israel. This was an extraordinary discretion indeed; the Israeli air force was based on French Mirage III's, Super-Mystères and Mystères.

Nasser the former failed law student was making juridical rationalizations of the inexplicable and fatal move by Nasser the flawed Arab who had seized the Strait of Tiran and closed it to Israeli shipping. "The claim that the Gulf of Aqaba is an international water-way is false," he said. This was a political oversimplification of a highly complicated legal point that was being argued by students of maritime and littoral law from Cairo to Harvard. Besides, it was irrelevant. Israel had already declared that the denial of the gulf—if that was what the Egyptians had really done—was an act of war.

The high-pitched voice echoed through the customs hall as passports were stamped and customs men scribbled with blue chalk on luggage. The implied prophecy of the *Economist* was switched on for a moment as Nasser reminded the press and the Egyptians listening to television and transistors that "the Soviet Union sided with our cause and it issued a communiqué saying that the Arab countries would not be alone, for the Soviet Union will also allow no intervention." Then the threat of world war vaporized in the hot air as Nasser the rational Weltpolitiker said that he didn't want a Middle Eastern conflict to become a confrontation between the United States and the Soviet Union. The winsome Nasser said that he had not permitted himself to think that the United States might actually go to war on Israel's side. If he considered such a thing, he said, "I would not proceed one inch forward." The hope of the Arab world said that Israel's very existence was a hostility.

If the press-conference statements, taken together, seemed contradictory, it was because the many parts of President Nasser were showing themselves. Like almost everything else that is human in the Arab world, he is far more intricate than the praise or expletives heaped upon him would indicate. That evening at the Nile Hilton there was a good deal of speculation among the Western correspondents about whom, exactly, Nasser was addressing in that press conference—Egypt, the Arab world or the whole world? Whoever it was, the Arabs of Cairo got the point they wanted to extract. An American traveler asked a man at the money-change cage what the President had said. The clerk smiled politely. "He says that we are very strong." The word had become fact again.

The road from the airport to Cairo leads out of wind-ruffled desert that is like a vast beach which never ends at water. A brown man with a white rag twisted around his head squatted on the center strip sprinkling a sapling with a garden hose while two goats and a bony dog looked on. In that dry universe of dust and white light the man, the animals and the task that absorbed them were a tableau of perfect futility.

Cairo announced itself with dun-colored compounds on its outskirts. These are said to be the houses of senior army officers and favored members of the higher intel-ligentsia; it is difficult to understand the desirability of real estate that fronts on the baking desert. Tall, dusty palm trees bent over roof terraces and grassless yards. Farther on, a long wall with barbed wire coiled along its top sheltered a big army camp that was both part of the Cairo garrison and a last staging area on the road to the Sinai. Soviet-built trucks, painted the color of the Egyptian earth, stood pointed toward the ominous des-ert to the east.

Other army trucks rattled and honked on the road into the city. The men driving them were bareheaded; their uniforms all looked like the castoffs of someone else's army.

The trucks and a few taxis were the only traffic on the roads. Friday is the Moslem Sabbath, but Christian colonialism's idle Sunday is a hard habit to break. Off the broad boulevards, on the narrower, shaded streets men dressed in the long, dirty smock called galabia sat on old chairs and listened to transistor radios. The press conference was still going on. If President Nasser's words were hotting up the furnace of Arab emotions, it didn't show in the eyes of the men of Cairo that evening. The only expression was the distant, lethargic melancholy of people who live in the sun. For a moment the impression was created that war was impossible because all human energy was needed just to keep the lungs and feet moving in that dolorous sargasso of heat and dirt. There is a special monotony of the spirit that hovers over poverty in arid places. The other side of Arabic melancholy is incoherent rage. Between them, humor and cordiality also exist. Wit is an Arab characteristic in the morning; by evening, numb sadness is the preface to sleep.

The Nile Hilton stands on the corniche, facing west. Egypt's river of life moves past the hotel, encumbered with the world's longest history and the color of military bean soup. The desk clerks—though they worked for a government-owned institution—seemed more a part of Conrad Hilton's grand design to smother the earth in American motel gothic than creatures of Egypt. Their skins were pale, their suits overly perfect in the Italian style, and their English grammar was impeccable. If the clerks had any opinions about the crisis or if they thought anything of the television camera crews, misplaced Japanese tourists or the Egyptian secret policemen in dark glasses who sat or walked about in the lobby, they were schooled to keep it to themselves.

The Western correspondents came back from the press conference after eight o'clock. The group included some of the best American reporters based in Europe.

The British contingent was dominated by a small army from the BBC. These people were looked upon with a special sort of gratitude by everyone else because, to the press, the BBC's morning broadcast in English was the link to the outside and therefore real world. There was an Egyptian-educated French correspondent who seemed to know everybody in Cairo.

The communist press lived somewhere else; nobody knew where, but it was presumed that they were quartered in some small, dirty, inexpensive and proletarian hotel. The only communist correspondent who mixed with his Western colleagues was a multi-lingual Yugoslav who was the object of some cultural curiosity because he also happened to be a Moslem.

The Nile Hilton was two-thirds empty. The tourists—except for the smiling, dogged Japanese who were determined to stay their allotted tour time come war, hell or high water—had all left on the advice of their embassies. American diplomatic families had been evacuated from Cairo and Alexandria. In the hotel promenade the shop-keepers spent most of the day looking out of the windows. Only the airline offices kept busy.

Dusk crossed Egypt and the correspondents moved, in groups, to dinner. The talk was serious but speculative. One was at the center of the crisis, but getting a feel for it was difficult. The center was a police state, the government operating things was omnipresent but inaccessible, and hardly anybody spoke Arabic. No one could define exactly the tone of President Nasser's press conference; by common agreement, it wasn't hysterical but it wasn't placatory either. Those who had talked with their offices in London or New York that evening had been told that Abba Eban, the foreign minister of Israel, had returned from his tour of major Western capitals and was reporting on his talks to the Israeli

Cabinet. To some of the correspondents, this made diplomacy seem still possible. To a few, it was inconceivable that the Americans would permit an Arab attack on Israel to go on for long. But that evening, as would be true all through the week in Cairo, neither the journalists nor the diplomats thought that the Arabs would move first. Nasser had won too much by his maneuvers so far; a war would be pointless from his perspective. Yet no one was completely sure that Nasser was in total control of events.

Darkness came down and the lights of the city sparkled in the Nile. Across the river, the Tower of Cairo was lit but empty. Egyptian engineering suffering, as it does, from an indifferent reputation, nobody wanted to dine in the revolving restaurant at the top of the tower. Farther down the river, a little minaret was silhouetted against the last red streaks of day. Over coffee and brandy the correspondents compared notes a final time.

However one cut the options, a magnet of intermeshing facts drew all opinion back to pessimism. Ninety thousand Egyptian troops were spread across the northern and central Sinai Desert. The Israeli forces were opposite them in the Negev. A definition of war had been drawn up in Tel Aviv: to deny Israel passage through the Gulf of Aqaba was an impermissible act of hostility. Nasser had apparently denied the gulf to Israel. The heat of the desert day, the cold of its night and the problems of supply and economics made the permanent deployment of such a vast force impossible for both sides. A mass had been put in place, the political momentum which motivated it had started, and the practical question was: could the mass move in any direction except forward?

Yet there is in almost every man a repository of secret reservation which makes him believe that the masters

of situations are in control of them. We look out upon
the world and our vision automatically arranges what it
perceives into systems of order. We believe, funda-
mentally, that the only real chaos is within ourselves. It
is only ourselves that we suspect of abandoning reason
for violence. War, that evening, still seemed improbable.

In contemplating a distant crisis, Europeans and
North Americans need to know, first of all, the identity
of the barbarians. Since Israel is a European presence
in the Middle East, it must follow that the Arabs are
the savages of the situation. As well as explaining nothing, this is also irrelevant in the totality of history. An
Arab prince boasted to T. E. Lawrence that there was a
mile of illuminated avenues in the Arab world when
Britons were still living in caves. One writer reminds us
that the Arabs were studying Aristotle at the same time
that Charlemagne was trying to figure out how to write
his own name.

It is impossible to consider the Arabs without assum-
ing the tragic view of history. There are several versions
of such a view. The European tragedy of history has
been set down by Jan Kott, the Polish critic, in his essay
on the historic dramas of Shakespeare:

In each of the Histories the legitimate ruler
drags behind him a long chain of crimes. He has
rejected the feudal lords who helped him to reach
for the crown; he murders, first, his enemies, then
his former allies; he executes possible successors
and pretenders to the crown. But he has not been
able to execute them all. From banishment a young
prince returns—the son, grandson, or brother of
those murdered—to defend the violated law. The
rejected lords gather round him, he personifies the

hope for a new order and justice. But every step to power continues to be marked by murder, violence, treachery. And so, when the new prince finds himself near the throne, he drags behind him a chain of crimes as long as that of the until now legitimate ruler. When he assumes the crown, he will be just as hated as his predecessor. He has killed enemies, now he will kill former allies. And a new pretender appears in the name of violated justice. The wheel has turned a full circle. A new chapter opens. A new historical tragedy . . .

In this tragic cycle of European history there is at least movement. The hope is offered us that one among the princes who ascend to power and guilt will manage to make the journey without totally corrupting himself. In the very turnover of dynasties there is the possibility of redemption.

This redemptory rhythm doesn't exist in the turgid, tragic history of the Arabs. Dynasties and colonial usurpers arise, imprint their particular lessons on the Arab character and then rot at the pinnacle of power, to be replaced as much by their own decay as by the aggressive ambitions of their successors.

From the beginning until Islam, the Arabic overture created a system of loyalties to small units—tribe or family; this sense of fidelity to an immediately visible and tangible unit sank to the red-gray strata of the mind where instincts and dreams have their origin. Then, as if to confuse that concept of loyalty, the Prophet Mohammed exploded into history toward the end of the sixth century with the only force that ever unified the Arabs —monotheism, a complex faith and practice that flow from a single God glorified by ninety-nine names. The Arabs coalesced and burst outward with such force that, one century after the Prophet's death, their empire rested on Transoxiana and northern India in the east and Spain in the west; if Charles Martel hadn't stopped them between Tours and Poitiers, it is conceivable that the Arabs might have established their great university, Al-Azhar, on the banks of the Thames at Oxford instead of beside the Nile at Cairo.

Through their operation of the empire, the Arabs displayed other aspects of their nature—so liberal in Islam's tolerance of its parent faiths, Judaism and Christianity, that the Jews of Spain rejoiced at first in the coming of the Moors; so uninterested in the techniques of government that the conquered peoples usually went on running their own affairs; so eclectic in art that Islam's second holiest shrine, the Dome of the Rock in Jerusalem, is regarded as a splendid bastardization of Greek and early Christian architecture. The empire was cosmopolitan. Nestorians tended the Arab caliphs as physicians, Persians painted their portraits and there were Christians among the viziers of Baghdad. To themselves the Moslem Arabs reserved the exclusive privilege of making war.

Perhaps an empire so dependent upon the people it conquered was doomed anyway. But the contradictions that history had already implanted in the Arabs were stalking their achievement; loyalty reverted back to house and tribe. The Ummayads never quite succeeded in establishing themselves as the true caliphs—successors—to the Prophet. They were ruthless and decadent in their luxurious courts at Damascus. The Abassids came out of the east and moved the center of the world to Baghdad. There the caliphs created the legendary splendor of the Arabian Nights while the individualism of the Arabs split Islam into half a dozen quarreling sects—Sunni, Shi'a, Hanifi, Alawi, Ismaili and the mysterious cult of Druze. The Abassids fell victim to the Turkish mercenaries they had hired to protect them from their brother Arabs. The collapse was not uniform. Samanids and Ghaznavids ascended in the east to form separatist Moslem dynasties while remnant Ummayads clung to Spain, and sundown came to the empire on invading waves of Turks, Mamelukes and Mongols, Christian Crusaders and then, finally, Ottoman Turks again. The glories of empire turned rancid in the collective memory and the Arabs became refugees from their own history, which shone behind them in perpetual reproach. At the same time, they blurred history to soften its pain. In his press conference President Nasser had asked those who listened to think back upon the fate of the Crusaders as an example of what the power of the Arabs could do to the usurpers of the Levant. "They have left," he said, "and what remains is a few fortresses which stand as mere monuments." But the historic truth is harsher and more complicated. Saladin, the genius who marshaled the forces of Islam against the Crusaders, was not an Arab but a Kurd, and the job was finished by Circassians from Central Asia.

The empire came apart at its center because its creators succumbed to the instinct for intra-familial warfare. But a vivid memory had burned itself into the minds of the desert people—Aiyamu-Arab, "the days of the Arabs," the ultimate moment of glory in which a culture accomplishes its own definition of virtue. The fact of the great conquest took its place beside the instinct for intimate loyalty and Islam's revelation of the possibilities of unity. The celebrated contradiction of the Arab mind had been founded.

Islam must be recognized as the force-majeur; the Arabs themselves become its vehicles, the executors of Islam's destiny. Aiyamu-Arab is really Aiyamu-Islam.

In the fourteenth century the Moslem historian Ibn Khaldun wrote that "the Arabs are incapable of founding an empire unless they are imbued with the religious enthusiasm of a prophet or a saint."

Yet glory, when considered by it previous possessors, becomes generalized. That which is Arabic created Islam, and Islam repaid the debt of its birth by creating the Arabs in history. From the seventh century until now the Arabs and Islam have been indivisible. When rot and opposition set upon the Ottoman empire in the nineteenth century and the British and the French began to colonize the Middle East, the ultimate question was contemplated by Arab radicals, nationalists and intellectuals: are the sources of the Arab renaissance in the past or should the Arabs forget history and throw themselves into the technological future implicit in the European colonizers? To this day the choices have never been resolved. The Arab socialism of Egypt and the Ba'athist doctrine of Syria are mixtures of past and future. The Arabs are bitter and guilty about the past and hate the Western sources of technology because they are reminders of the humiliations of nineteenth-century colonialism. The Arab imagination, said T. E. Lawrence, is "vivid but not creative." So, the reconciliation of the past and a hated stranger's technology being impossible, a final layer was placed upon the strata of history that had formed the Arab character: immeasurable inner conflict, destructive and profound.

On Monday, May 29, the sun blasted Cairo with simmering, eye-crippling heat and the radio stations of the Middle East were crying havoc. Kol Israel, in Hebrew, broadcast Prime Minister Eshkol's speech to the Knesset. "Egypt's moves constitute a threat to peace in our entire region. The Egyptian President's inflammatory declarations and threats are creating illusions among his supporters, who are easy to inflame with passion. The ruler of Egypt ought to remember that this is not the first time he was carried away by his imagination and saw himself as the victor before he had set out for battle." Eshkol was fighting on two fronts—against the Knesset militants represented by David Ben-Gurion and Moshe Dayan, who implied that the Prime Minister was corrupting Israel's self-reliance by too much reliance on diplomacy, and also in a battle of serious words against the Arabs.

In Arabic, Cairo Radio broadcast President Nasser's speech to a delegation of the National Assembly which had visited him at noon. "We are confronting Israel and the West as well," he said, "the West which created Israel and which despised us, the Arabs, and which ignored us before and after 1948." He ended in a burst of ferocious piety: "May God help us and grant us success in restoring conditions to what they were before 1948!" The Assemblymen applauded handsomely.

Nasser, at this point, appeared to be fighting on two fronts also. One was represented by that side of his own nature which is capable of rational assessment of all given elements in a situation. The other front was composed of the excitement that the crisis had generated in the Arab world at large, Syria's dangerous goading of the equally if differently aroused Israelis and the burden of dominating events that popular adulation and destiny had imposed upon Nasser's character.

There are three mysteries in the origins of the third Arab-Israeli war. The first is the motive of the Syrian government. It had come to power in an especially gory coup d'état in February 1966 and was composed, at the top, of a few men with the curious combination of medical and Marxist educations. The President of Syria,

Dr. Nourredin El Atassi, is a heavy, scowling person in the first reaches of middle age with a reported history of manic depression. Although it claims the inheritance of the confusing political doctrines of Ba'ath (whose founding prophet, Michel Aflak, the El Atassi group had expelled from Syria), the government of Damascus was more rooted in the orthodox left than any other government of the Middle East. Its speeches were filled with the gritty semantics of Marxism and it never evoked God. The Syrians had attracted all sorts of favorable attention and assistance from Moscow. The guerrilla-war theories of Mao Tse-tung, General Giap and Che Guevara are enormously appealing to the movers and shakers of Damascus, and they regarded the annihilation of Israel as a proletarian if not holy duty. The imperatives of God can be talked about indefinitely without acting upon them; for years Nasser had been warning other Arab leaders that the time was not right for an attack on Israel. The imperatives of Marx apparently can't wait.

Immediately upon coming to power, the new government in Damascus activated El Fatah, one of the network of organizations set up to do sabotage inside Israel's borders. El Fatah and its commando wing, El Assifa—"The Storm"—were largely made up of Palestinian refugees, the hapless Arab residents of Palestine who fled, were expelled or were lured out by Arab governments when Israel was created in 1948. El Assifa had been conducting sporadic raids ever since its creation in 1964. After the new Syrian government had established itself in Damascus, El Assifa went to work in earnest. From Syria, Lebanon and across the long, loosely administered Jordanian border with Israel, guerrillas made twenty-eight raids into Jewish territory in the first ten months of 1965. By 1967 the tempo had increased to the rate of thirteen raids between March and May from the Syrian-Lebanese frontier and eight across the border from Jordan. The attacks varied from setting off bombs in the middle of an Israeli crowd at a football match to blowing water stations and bridges, derailing trains, mining roads and shooting up villages.

The effect, in Israel, was to generate an exasperated and understandable public militance. This became, eventually, the source of General Moshe Dayan's immense public popularity on the eve of the war. The effect of Syrian policy in the Arab world was a bit more complicated. Though Jordan and Egypt publicly applauded the activities of El Assifa (but not the terrorists' Syrian sponsors), the raids created bitter hostility between Damascus and Amman, the capital of the more moderate Hashemite King of Jordan. When Israel replied to one of the Jordan-based El Assifa raids in November 1966 by sending a tank column into the village of Es Sammu, evacuating the inhabitants and blowing up forty houses, King Hussein was outraged. The monarchical Jordanians had been going through a particularly bad patch with the socialist Egyptians in the endless, mordant nattering of the Arab world's rival politics. Hussein publicly demanded an explanation of why Nasser had not sent help when the Israelis hit Jordan. Amman Radio accused the Egyptians of "hiding behind the skirts of United Nations legality"—a reference to the U.N. Emergency Force that had sat between the Egyptians and the Israelis in the Sinai for ten years.

The effect in Cairo of Syria's dangerous cavortings around Israel was to pose the possibility of a serious military collision. On the evidence of what he had said in private and implied in public, President Nasser thought that war with Israel would probably be a loser's exercise for the Arabs. (On May 26 he had addressed

an Arab trade-union delegation and had more or less
admitted that his approach to the Israelis had been cautious for quite some time. In referring to the coming
struggle, he said, "The battle will be a general one and
our basic objective will be to destroy Israel. I probably
could not have said such things five or even three years
ago. If I had said such things and had been unable to
carry them out, my words would have been empty and
valueless. Today, some eleven years after 1956, I say
such things because I am confident.") Had Israel suddenly attacked Syria, Nasser could not have stood by
and watched. He was in the uncomfortable position of
having his foreign and military policy put into forced
march by a government in Damascus whose views of
the world were doctrinaire rubbish and whose leader's
mental condition was questionable.

At the same time the tensions stirred up by Syria had
churned and excited the old anti-Israel passions of the
Arab world in general. In the land of the aggrieved, he
who seizes the banner first is the leader. The Syrian
banner was shaped and colored like a bloody shirt; the
solution of the Jewish question as Damascus presented
it was the well-known final one. On Independence Day
the previous spring President El Atassi had made the
point as clearly as the vaporous jargon of Syrian Marxism permitted: "Through their past experiences in the
struggle and their fight against all imperialist forces, our
people have become convinced that the all-out people's
war of liberation is the only road to the liberation of
Palestine and the smashing of imperialist and reactionary plans." Undressed of its rhetoric, this was exciting
stuff indeed for millions of Arabs. Placed against Syria's
ferocious light, President Nasser had begun to look a
little pale. He was slipping and Damascus was taking
the play.

It was exactly at the confluence of these several dilemmas that the second great mystery of the whole crisis occurred. With the Middle East drenched in the petrol of passion and uncertainty, the Soviet Union decided to light a match.

On May 13 the Soviet embassies in Cairo and Damascus had told the two Arab governments that Soviet intelligence had conclusive evidence that an Israeli attack on Syria was imminent—not a border raid but a major assault designed to bring down the government in Damascus.

Nothing has subsequently come to light to indicate that this was true. No other serious intelligence service in the world claims to have discovered the evidence that the Soviets were talking about—and Israel is a veritable specimen slide under the scrutiny of all sorts of intelligence agencies, friendly and hostile alike. Premier Eshkol later offered to take the Soviet ambassador to Tel Aviv into the region north of the Sea of Galilee to see for himself if Israeli forces were massed there for a jump into Syria (the ambassador said he didn't need to go and look; with the dogged faith that small children have in their fathers and the ambassadors of autocracies ostensibly have in their governments, the Soviet emissary said that if Moscow said it, it must be so) and the Secretary General of the United Nations issued a report saying there was no proof of any Israeli massing near the Syrian border.

There is some dispute about when and how this report was given to Egypt and Syria. President Nasser claimed that it was passed to an Egyptian parliamentary delegation that visited Moscow in May. If this were so, the report of an impending Israeli attack on Syria might have been part of the general verbiage exchanged on the occasion of such a parliamentary visit. By the same token, the report given in such a fashion would not have inspired the Egyptians to anything more than a fresh eruption of propaganda attacks on the perfidy of the Israelis. Nor would the United Nations have gone to the lengths it did to deny the allegations of an Israeli massing in and around Rosh Pinna and the area to the north. There is a good deal of evidence that the report *was* passed from the Soviet embassies in Cairo and Damascus on Saturday, May 13, and that the diplomats presenting it to the Egyptians and the Syrians quoted Soviet intelligence as the supporting source.

The Egyptians apparently believed the Russians and were alarmed. In describing the way he operates, President Nasser has often said, "I never act, I only react." The time had obviously come to tone down the Syrians and—if the Soviet report were true—to divert the Israelis from the north and draw their attention and forces toward the Sinai. On the evening of May 14 the Israelis picked up the signs of Egyptian troop movement. That day the Egyptian chief of staff, General Mohammed Fawzi, flew to Damascus to confer with Syrian military leaders. On May 15 the Egyptian armed forces were put on alert. By the 16th they were moving into the desert. Nasser had reacted.

At this point U Thant dashed upon the stage like the Tyl Eulenspiegel of diplomacy. On May 18 President Nasser asked the United Nations to remove some of its Emergency Force troops from several positions in the Sinai and to send them back to the U.N.E.F. camp in the Gaza Strip for their own safety. He was making a grandstand reply to the Jordanian charges of cowering behind the United Nations. In his May 18 request Nasser said nothing about taking the U.N.E.F. troops out of Sharm El Sheik, the outpost that commanded the Strait of Tiran leading to the Gulf of Aqaba.

U Thant conferred in New York with ambassadors of the nations supplying the Emergency Force troops and then came up with an extraordinary policy. It was, in effect, all or nothing. Either the whole U.N. force stayed or it cleared out of all its Sinai positions, including Sharm El Sheik. Thant flew to Cairo for talks with President Nasser, stayed one day less than he had planned and returned to the United Nations. To astonished diplomats all over the world it appeared that the Secretary General of the United Nations had fallen prey to a fever of petulance. One foreign minister lamented that the U.N.—which often maddens with its slowness of action—was now maddening with a display of capricious speed. Like the legendary German prankster, U Thant came and went, and the main event resumed, only slightly altered by his presence. His action uncorked a festering bottle that probably would have blown its cork in time anyway.

What is extraordinary about the Soviet report—aside from its remoteness from the truth—is its violation of the fundamental principle of Soviet policy in the Middle East. Historically, there is a long tradition of Russian interest and interference in the region. The Middle East presents to the Russians more or less the same alarms and temptations that Latin America does to the United States—it is potentially rich, periodically unstable and not too far away. Catherine the Great conducted all sorts of maneuvers and skulduggery around Turkey, and Napoleon conceded Russia's right to pick on Persia when he signed the Treaty of Tilsit.

Obviously, communism should have problems in a part of the world whose principal homogeneous feature is a great religion. But ideological inconsistencies have never been a serious obstacle to Soviet national ambitions. The fact that Israel is the only belligerent in the

June 5 war which permits the existence of an indigenous communist party may be fodder for contemplation by the gloomy ironists of the Soviet collegium. But it says nothing to Soviet foreign policy. Russia voted in the United Nations to create Israel, her propaganda organisms have been flailing hell out of the Jewish state ever since, while her diplomatic relations with Tel Aviv have been passable.

For all of her generalized noise in support of the Arabs—and for all the Soviet arming of Arab states, too —Moscow has conducted herself with considerable prudence on the specifics of the Middle East. The first Soviet principle is to make sure that the conflicts and partisanships of the area don't get so far out of control that the Soviet Union finds itself face to face with the United States—the Russians in support of their revolutionary Arabs and the United States backing its kings and Jews. For this reason the Russians have never urged the Arabs to go to war against Israel. Politically, the Soviets are all for rooting the United States and the United Kingdom out of the Middle East. They support President Nasser's anti-colonialism as a principle and applaud the Egyptian drive to get the British out of Aden. But the Russians don't necessarily want President Nasser to be the one to replace Harold Wilson in southern Arabia. In the early summer of 1967 the Soviet-sponsored National Liberation Front in Aden seemed to be elbowing aside the Egyptians' Front for the Liberation of South Yemen in the bloody campaign against the British.

In late March Andrei Gromyko visited Cairo for talks with President Nasser that were officially described as involving "various discussions." There is no evidence that Gromyko did any inciting on the Israeli issue—in fact, there is some evidence to the contrary. The Egyptian newspaper *Al Ahram* said that Mr. Gromyko had encouraged President Nasser in his moribund war in the Yemen. The Soviet embassy in Cairo immediately circulated a swatch of rumors that the Soviet foreign minister had, in fact, told Nasser to take it easy in the Yemen. Russia is not especially keen on having the Egyptians get into an intractable tangle with the American-backed Saudi monarchy.

The Soviet Union began to sell weapons to Egypt and Syria with the celebrated Czech arms deal of 1955. Later, Algeria and Iraq became Russian clients in weaponry. By the late spring of 1967 the Egyptian air force was equipped with, among other things, 360 fighter planes—the advanced MIG-21 as well as the earlier but very efficient MIG-17 and MIG-19. The weapons that Egypt rolled into the desert in the middle of May included nearly two thirds of the 1,300 tanks that the Russians had sold to her. Seven Soviet-built Egyptian destroyers steamed back and forth in the Mediterranean and the Red Sea. Soviet advisers had trained the Egyptians and Syrians in more than just the handling of Russian weapons; the basic Egyptian conformation in the Sinai was along the design of Soviet strategy—a two-level defense and an obvious reliance on masses of troops in the event of hostilities.

In supplying weapons to the Egyptians and Syrians and the other socialist Arab states, the Soviets ran four basic risks. First, the weapons might be used for purposes that the Soviets didn't intend; in 1963 Moscow threatened to cancel military aid to Iraq because the Iraqis were using their Soviet arms to fight the Kurds and Moscow is pro-Kurd. Second, there is the risk that the weapons could start something that would lead on to a Soviet-American showdown. Third, the great masses of weapons might overburden the fragile economies of the recipient states, thus creating a need for emergency Soviet financial assistance and slowing down the development of socialist economies which is one of the collateral Soviet objectives in the Middle East. Fourth, there might be a revolt—not an uncommon feature of Arab political life—and the weapons could fall into the wrong hands.

With some minor variations, these are the same risks that the United States, the United Kingdom and France were running in their policies of arming the Israelis, Saudi Arabia and Jordan. The sale of weapons is a curious but understandably effective way of winning unstable friends and influencing angry people. In a tragic closed circle of great-power policy, weapons-flogging can always be rationalized by the explanation that the nasty others are doing it, too.

In terms of economic assistance, the Soviets tend to regard Egypt as a bottomless pit—though the Russians were delighted to take over the bills and technology of the High Aswan Dam after Secretary Dulles, in a spasm of international morality, ended American assistance to the project. At one point Moscow urged President Nasser not to push things so far with the Americans that U.S. grain shipments under P.L. 480 would be cut off. Unhappily, the President of Egypt didn't pay close attention to this particular Soviet advice. Just as unhappily, he took the loony Soviet report of an impending attack on Syria at face value, to his own and subsequent Russian grief.

Not all of this was apparent by any means to the correspondents sunning themselves and swatting flies at the Nile Hilton swimming pool on the blistering morning of May 29. They were in a frustrating position; having come from all over the world to cover a crisis, they couldn't get their hands on it. President Nasser and his circle were moving at the center of the universe, but no one had any way of gauging their mood, feelings or plans. There weren't even many rumors to check out or ignore. The Egyptian government was everywhere—its propaganda posters were draped all over the dirty, sweltering city and speculation about its thoughts dominated the minds of the reporters—but the government was invisible. It was rather like covering Moscow, where under normal circumstances the only sources of information are the public utterances of the regime and the views of various diplomats.

The embassies of Cairo were in several stages of communication with the Egyptian government—none of them very satisfactory. The Soviets were in touch on all the levels of their military and diplomatic involvement with the Egyptians, but they hadn't been told everything by a long shot. When correspondents went around to see them, Russian diplomats shrugged, put on displays of sarcastic indignation about the United States, Britain and Israel and protested that the crisis had nothing to do with them. But there was an undercurrent of anxiety in all of the blather. After the war was over, a Soviet diplomat in New York, well oiled with Vat 69 and rue, said, suddenly, "How could we have been so stupid?" His colleagues in Cairo the week before the fighting broke out had, perhaps, intimations that Soviet policy in the Middle East had gone all wobbly. At that point the Russians, like everybody else, were studying with ever darkening vision the third mystery of the crisis, President Nasser's move on the Gulf of Aqaba. In Cairo they swore—and the estimates of Western powers after the war tended to confirm—that Moscow had not been consulted about the Aqaba caper in advance; its implications were terrifying. In the United Nations the same week the Soviet ambassador, Nikolai Federenko, was sounding as if he had taken leave of his senses. His accusation that the Israelis were behaving in a "Hitlerian" manner will go down in history as one of diplomacy's vulgar non-sequiturs. The belligerence of Mr. Federenko and of the Soviet diplomats in Cairo was that of the boy who has accidentally killed the cat when nobody was looking and has decided to plead outraged innocence to the gathered crowd.

The American embassy was tormenting itself with a bout of diplomatic fratricide and was as isolated from the Egyptian government as the reporters at the Hilton swimming pool. The American ambassadorship had been rotated, Lucius Battle leaving in March to become Assistant Secretary of State for Near Eastern and South Asian Affairs—a post that had been vacant since the previous November. The new ambassador was Richard Nolte, a young and scholarly Arabist without any diplomatic experience. In the interim between Battle's departure and Nolte's arrival the embassy had been in the hands of David G. Nes, a Foreign Service career officer. Nes, like most other diplomats in Cairo, had been alarmed by the atmosphere in the Egyptian capital during April and May. At the same time he had apparently developed the idea that his dispatches warning of trouble to come were being ignored in the State Department and the White House. (They weren't. The administration was at its wits' end over both the Middle East situation and the refusal of a pious and oversimplifying Congress to sanction a return to P.L. 480 wheat shipments for Egypt.) Nes's belief that he was being ignored prompted him to write a letter to Senator William Fulbright, the chairman of the Senate Foreign Relations Committee. This irritated the State Department, which conveyed its irritation back to the chargé d'affaires in Cairo—thereby adding a feeling of being put upon to Nes's understandable anxieties over the crisis.

On May 21, Ambassador Nolte arrived in Cairo and was met at the airport by a group of Western and Egyptian reporters. When he was asked what he thought about the crisis, the new ambassador—addressing himself to the Egyptian press, answered, "What crisis?" While the envoy's phrasing may have persuaded Egyptian reporters that Washington was not losing control of itself, the effect on Mr. Nes could not have been a reassuring one. A certain chill developed between the new ambassador and the former chargé.

Immediately after Nolte's arrival the situation took its worst turn to date; on May 22, President Nasser made his speech at an air base in the Sinai Desert announcing the apparent blockade of the Gulf of Aqaba. It was this enigmatic but fatal gesture which led Israel to charge that an act of war had taken place. On instruction from his government, the new American ambassador went to see Mahmoud Riyad, the Egyptian foreign minister. What transpired at that meeting became the subject of confusion and controversy; a faintly absurd verbal game of who-struck-John was added to the general din of official invective that preceded the war. Nolte had some papers with him, including one that reviewed American policy on the rights of innocent passage in 1957, but his message to the foreign minister was simple and verbal. The United States wanted Egypt and everybody else to please, for God's sake, take it easy while diplomacy had a chance to cool things down. Riyad later claimed that Nolte had given him a paper and had threatened the use of force by the United States unless the Aqaba blockade was lifted. This was picked up and trumpeted by the Egyptian press in line with President Nasser's claims that the enemy was not only Israel but the American-led West as well.

Then Ambassador Nolte held what is known as a "backgrounder" for American reporters in Cairo. This is a meeting which conveys official information that is not supposed to be attributed to official sources. At the backgrounder Ambassador Nolte was asked if he had in fact threatened Mr. Riyad. The ambassador's answer was ambivalent enough to leave a fragment of doubt which was translated by one news agency (but not by its correspondent present at the meeting) into an affirmation of what Riyad was saying. The State Department's reaction was bafflement and dismay; its embassy in Cairo appeared to have somehow got out of control. The Department dispatched Charles W. Yost, a former ambassador to Syria, to see what was going on in Cairo.

The American embassy's reaction to itself and to the press was to stop co-operating with reporters. The correspondents in Cairo were in the odd position of being talked to and even entertained by the embassies of other countries, including Russia, but not by the Americans. The press attaché, a correct and nervous young man named Garcia, told visiting newsmen that he didn't know anything . . . including the reasons for Yost's visit. The embargo on candor went on until the middle of the week before the war, when Robert Bauer, the sensible Austrian-born public-affairs officer, persuaded the American embassy to relax a little. Two American correspondents had a further go at Ambassador Nolte, who said that he hadn't threatened Riyad at all: their conversation, in fact, had been very pleasant.

The French embassy in Cairo—unlike America's—had been in contact with President Nasser on and off during the crisis, apparently at Nasser's own instigation. There was nothing precise in the exchanges. The time for negotiation, said French diplomats, had not yet arrived. Paris was also keeping its lines open in Tel

Aviv. The press attaché of the French embassy in Cairo, Jean-Pierre Guyot, was a slender, prematurely bald young man with a graceful and precise mind who seemed to be everywhere in the city; his daily rounds included the offices of the Western news agencies and the Hilton, where he appeared twice a day. Guyot became the barometer for the reporters who talked to him. The situation each morning was either "gonflé" or "dégonflé"—inflated or deflated.

Officially, the British didn't exist in Cairo. The Egyptians had broken relations with the United Kingdom over Rhodesia. The British embassy was still operating with a skeleton crew as the "British interest section" of the Canadian embassy. The British compound off the corniche was hollow and dignified. Most of the Egyptian staff had departed and a counselor manned the reception desk. London's diplomatic unpersons in Cairo— including a blonde secretary of astonishing good looks —were cool and amusing about their extremely vulnerable situation. The British had a long history in Egypt— not all of it liberal or savory—and their acquired instincts made things look ominous to them. Like most other Westerners, the British didn't think that the Egyptians would attack first. President Nasser had accomplished too much with the situation to date to blow his achievements in a war.

The Italians were cool in Cairo, too. They were liked by the Egyptians—indeed, there was an erroneous general impression in the Middle East that the Italians were pro-Arab in the crisis—and they appeared to understand the temper of Cairo. Their guesses and estimates of the situation were reliable, and Italians had performed some discreet and modestly useful diplomacy in Rome, New York and Cairo. But their access to the government was limited.

The remotest of all the embassies was that of the People's Republic of China. It appeared to exist as an organic extension of China, complete in and of itself, rather than as a representative mission to the Egyptian government. Bottled up in a baroque old mansion behind high walls, the Chinese were too busy conducting a Great Proletarian Cultural Revolution among the embassy staff members to take much notice of the Arab-Israeli crisis. From time to time the neighborhood heard squeals and thumps from the Chinese compound as the resolute pursuit of revisionism went on in faithful imitation of the main event in Peking.

In the heat of the day, the carrion-picking kites soared and curved in the sky above the scattered city; they were looking for rotted edibles, and even the center of Cairo seemed full of them. The east bank of the Nile, where most commerce and activity takes place, is crisscrossed with side streets where venders sell fruit juice in smudged bottles and dry little pastries are displayed on sheets of metal stacked on old wooden counters. Uneaten bits are thrown into the streets. Barefoot children in dirty galabias play and urinate on the worn cobbles or sprawl in the sudden sleep of heat exhaustion on old wagon beds or under chairs. The excrement of dray horses so thin that their capacity to defecate is a minor wonder lies in dry, fly-swarming heaps against the curbs. Cars park half on the sidewalk and half in the street, wooden carts are jammed between them, and cadaverous dogs sniff at the sources of the general rot which permeates the stifling, motionless air.

The main boulevards are cleaner simply because so much is moving on them. The taxis of Cairo are all little black-and-white Mercedes which move in lunging herds among trucks, wandering people and private cars; the taxis rush at any space that opens up in the traffic. Their drivers blast horns, shout greetings back and forth and curse to themselves when their folly is frustrated by the follies of other drivers. The traffic, for some reason, seems to stay off the corniche. The road running along the Nile is always maneuverable; the handsomest new buildings of Cairo are on the corniche, too—the Hilton, the TV building and the skeletal beginnings of a curved structure intended for offices. None of these buildings is tall by the standards of London or Rome and certainly not by comparison with New York's astronomic heights, but they tower over the rest of Cairo. The Egyptian capital is low and its predominant color is a yellowish buff. From the Agence France-Presse bureau thirteen floors high, the roofs of Cairo look like a series of uneven stairs that can't make up their minds whether to go up or down.

Away from the brief stretch of modern façade on the corniche, Cairo's east-bank structure evokes the colonial style of the nineteenth century; windows are shuttered against the heat and light, yellow walls flake plaster and up under the eaves Victorian baroque trim choked with dirt coils its way around four sides. Even the great Cairo Museum, constructed of brown stone with a green metal dome in the middle of its roof, looks as if it had been built for a turn-of-the-century exposition in Paris.

In the dark, cool halls of the museum the funerary art of Egypt has arrested for all time the faces of people who inhabited the longest history in the world. Quite apart from the remembered glories of the race that has populated her since the Arab conquest in the seventh century, Egypt has this other history which goes back so far that the land of the Nile was literally the only civilized country on earth at one time.

In a roughly carved intaglio relief a woman of the tenth dynasty lifts her hands to her head in eternal mourning; King Osorkon III of Libya is caught in carved stone as he leans forward, head raised, to launch a ceremonial barge; from the eighteenth or early nineteenth dynasty Naia, the wife and sister of Thay, stares out at infinity with adolescent dignity; the tragic, visionary King Akhenaton and his family are portrayed in bas-relief as spidery figures making offerings to the sun god Aton—Akhenaton found monotheism, too, but Aton destroyed him; the famous head of Nefertiti is in a German museum, but there is another and better one in Cairo that coaxes the queen's fragile grace out of porous stone; she shares the exalted summit of physical perfection with the goddesses of Joy and Peace from the pyramid of King Sahure and with the slender nude figure of a woman holding a lotus, carved in the fifth dynasty. Thutmosis I has the face of a king in love. There are a perfect little blue hippopotamus, a flock of geese and a man milking a cow. Soldiers march, boatmen fight, dwarfs dance and a woman bends to drink from a fatal river in a painting from one of the Books of the Dead.

These people who have come forward through the smoky centuries to present themselves to us in wood, stone and paint knew something. It is in a bemused expression of wisdom and tranquillity that glows from their faces. Perhaps because they made the greatest journey of all—from barbarism to society—the thing that they knew was as simple as the fact that they were the beginning. They were the residents of the first chamber of civilization, and perhaps it was the best one. In the carvings they made no attempt to hide the darker side of their epochs. They fought wars to conquer territory and take prisoners, and the prisoners became slaves. The people were cruel and unjust, and death was so immense all around them that they made a cult of it, created their art as an offering to the cult and, thus, gave themselves permanent life in the witness of all the centuries that followed them. We have not managed to purge ourselves of the sins of war, cruelty and injustice despite the advantage of having evolved through the subsequent millennia, yet we don't know what they knew.

The three million Copts of Egypt claim to be the only descendants of the early civilization. The other twenty-seven million Egyptians—and they increase at the rate of a million a year—are a combination of races, all answering, in the careless categorization of contemporary politics, to the name of Arab. ("Anyone who speaks Arabic as his mother tongue is an Arab," Nasser has said.) In contrast to the violent, spastic motions of the traffic, the pedestrians of Cairo move like sleepwalkers. During the week before the war the city was strung with banners and posters exhorting the people to the holy fervor that would annihilate Israel and the damnable imperialists in the blood-fire of righteous Arab rage and bring back Aiyamu-Arab on a screeching wave of MIG-21's. The squiggly script of proclamatory Arabic printed in red and black upon the banners that stretched across the streets and hung from buildings added to the chaotic impression of Cairo's traffic and wandering masses. But the written word and the harangues broadcast from street-corner loudspeakers did not seem to penetrate past the anesthetic of heat and the accumulations of secret misery imprinted upon the faces of the people in the streets. They encompass some of the world's most beautiful faces and some of its ugliest. There were striking, erect Nubians, the gentle, faithful blacks from the depths of the interior; desert Arabs with burned, creased faces; country women in black shawls that covered dully flowered shirts and bare, square feet; Arab men from the cities and the coast in the inevitably dirty galabia which looks like a long nightshirt; small

men with the fierce beauty of Semitism in their features
and others whose eyes, noses and curved mouths evoked
the historic Greek entanglement in the races and
thoughts of Egypt. There were blue-eyed Caucasians
from the Delta, pale and better-dressed than the others,
soldiers in uniforms that had been worn to a pale gray-
buff; many of them looked to be no more than boys. In
the common denominator of military dress they ranged
from Negroes through the round brown faces of Arabs
to Europeans. Eight days later when a group of reporters wandered among the Egyptian dead in the Sinai
they would see the color differential resolved into the
sun-scorched black of lifeless flesh. Among the living
crowds of Cairo the color contrast has been compro-
mised in some faces that mix all the other races together;
they are red-haired, blue-eyed and their skins are the
tone of potash.

The loudspeakers shrieked, the banners proclaimed;
but none among the intended audience appeared to take
any notice. Everything in Arab life exists on two levels
at least. War and the special hope it symbolizes for the
Arabs were whooping from the skies, but nobody
smiled; the melancholy of the second half of the day was
spreading. The eye of the observer in the streets of Cairo
pleads for a relieving splash of bright color, a red, a
green or a blue. The dull tones seem to be deliberately
worn to cloak the bright phobias and obsessions that
are the inner vestment of the Arabs. Islam puts sharp
limits on its children's intoxicants. Words take the place
of alcohol, and intricate sexuality is the secret esthetic
which relieves the misery of life. Both come at a certain
price—illusion, war and too many children.

A few hours later some of the correspondents saw the
reverse side of Arab melancholy—the terrifying verbal
rage of Cairo's mobs.

The offices of United Press International are on one of the unkempt little side streets. The visitor has to climb three flights of a dark, gritty stairway, past obscenities and telephone numbers scribbled on the walls. He crosses landings where brass plates on closed doors proclaim in Arabic and English the practices of an optometrist and a lawyer.

Two men sit in the bare outer office of the UPI suite fingering a copy of the afternoon newspaper spread on a table before them. They are part of that immense army of Middle Eastern males whose function in life is to sit in the anterooms of the usefully employed, run errands and fetch little cups of bitter black coffee. They half rise, smile at the visitor and say something incomprehensible that is meant as welcome.

Farther in, teletype machines are set around another high-ceilinged room that is also cluttered with a news desk and two other tables. The news on the late afternoon of May 29 wasn't very hopeful. The speeches that Premier Eshkol and President Nasser had made earlier in the day were being fed back from the central desks in London and New York as exemplars of the deteriorating situation. The wires were running double-entry analyses of the relative military strengths of Israel and her Arab enemies. The Israelis seemed to be outnumbered in almost everything that rolled, flew or fired. Even their superior drive and skill assumed from the victories of 1948 and 1956 were now open to question, according to the potted military analyses written in Europe and North America. The Egyptians had had years of battle testing and experience in the Yemen. The Soviets had equipped and trained the armies of Egypt; the analysts assumed that the dauntless military spirit of Russia could be transferred to the Arabs by the teaching of her techniques and the donation of her weapons, and they overlooked the somewhat embarrassing reality that huge Egyptian armies which sometimes included up to 65,000 men equipped with all the electronic paraphernalia of contemporary combat had been stalemated for nearly five years against the faintly absurd tribal guerrillas of the Imam El-Badr. The Yemeni war was a bloody game of hide-and-seek fought in the arid northern hills of an ancient land. The coming battle with Israel was to be old-fashioned and brutally simple—us against them and no place to hide.

The wires were also reporting that afternoon that an Egyptian patrol in the Sinai had wandered by accident across Israeli lines and had been captured. Its members —including a senior officer—were being interrogated.

Word had come through several of the UPI's Egyptian staff that a big war rally was going to be held that evening in a working-class district of Cairo. Several Western correspondents set off for the television building to do their evening broadcasts before going on to the rally.

There was no censorship in Cairo the week before the war; in one sense, censorship can be a comfort to reporters working in a police state. It defines exactly how far a journalist can go. His indiscretions are penciled out before he makes them. The regime, by doing this, persuades itself that it has maintained its best image abroad. For the reporter the censorship process is really an illusion; in a land of no justice it doesn't do much good to try to obey the rules—they can pick you up any time they want and do anything to you they wish on any pretext. But the censored reporter at least has the illusory comfort that he can't be nailed for his words printed and broadcast abroad. The regime has already concurred in their transmission.

In Cairo that week something—perhaps it was just

the general atmosphere of hostility toward the West—implied to the correspondents that they were free to say anything they liked providing they didn't go too far and the definition of too far was their problem, not the Egyptian government's. In the second-floor studios of Radio Cairo there was a big control room where circuits were plugged in and bookings made. The staff were helpful and courteous. Behind little glass panels, tape recorders were visible, turning slowly, recording—it seemed obvious—everything that went out on the air to London and New York. Broadcast correspondents always assume that somewhere in the bowels of the radio stations of dictatorships the tape recorders are taking down everything they say. To actually see them alerts the mind marvelously.

Part of the semantic game in Cairo that week was the sensible rule that the name Israel was never mentioned when travel plans were discussed in hotel rooms or restaurants—which were bugged—or on broadcast circuits abroad. The correspondents in Egypt used the code name "Dixie" for Israel, but it took their editors on the other end of the circuits some days to work out what the men in Cairo were talking about when they mentioned departure dates for Dixie. It appeared that Alabama should brace itself for an influx of Arabic-oriented writers. (The Cairo correspondents of the Westinghouse Broadcasting Company worked under a special uneasiness. They were afraid of getting signed cables from the company's chief operating officer, whose name was Israel.) The Dixie synonym probably didn't fool the Egyptians a bit, but it, too, was an illusory comfort.

After finishing their circuits, the correspondents drove off to the district where the rally was going to take place. The neighborhood—not the poorest in Cairo by any means—was gray, slatternly and, characteristically, made up of low, disintegrating buildings. Shallow shops and coffee houses lined the avenue displaying fly-covered rows of pastry and meats, lines of unglazed pottery and baskets stacked in leaning towers. Old wooden chairs had been placed on the sidewalks outside the coffee houses. Men sat in the dusk looking out across the boulevard. Many of them appeared to be wearing carpet slippers. Small, black-shrouded women moved along the sidewalks, but never sat down on the chairs. One old person squatted by the corner of a shop while two children who seemed to be too young to have come from her played at the curb; the old woman had the face of an exhausted bird. Nearby a square-faced mother sat against a wall nursing a baby from one enormous breast thrust out of the dirty folds of her black clothing.

Across the avenue a wooden archway stood over the entrance to a side street. It was draped with banners imprinted with flaming red letters of Arabic like bloody worm-tracks. Beyond the archway a loudspeaker system blared martial music into the hot evening. Superimposed upon this ear-denting din was the high, cutting rhetoric of an agitator; he spoke in rhythmic bursts which assumed a contrapuntal cadence to the military music. The street on the other side of the archway was darker than the boulevard and it was filled with people.

Feeling a mixture of curiosity, apprehension and exhilaration at their own boldness, the correspondents crossed the boulevard. Members of a camera crew were coming out carrying their equipment. They had to get the film onto a New York flight, they said. The correspondents asked them how it was inside. Great pictures, the crew answered. Wild.

The side street had been barricaded two blocks down

by a wooden stand built of rough timbers and draped—walls, floor and a ceiling—with imitation Persian carpets. Facing it, all down the street to the archway, thousands of people stood or squatted in rows. The buildings on both sides were so rickety that they appeared about to collapse on the packed crowd beneath them. Every window, door and balcony was stuffed with human beings; others stood crowded on the edges of the roofs and even hung perilously from drainpipes, bracing their feet on window sills. Banners were draped across the street from wall to wall, and loudspeakers had been fixed to poles and door jambs to convey the words and music from the stand to every ear in the two-block area. Paper lanterns hung among the banners, and floodlights burned down, attracting flies by the thousands. The noise was like an inundating sea. The crowd swayed; the agitator shouted a burst of angry, soaring phrase and the crowd yelled it back to him; the phrase in rich choleric Arabic bellowed from the loudspeakers again, and again the crowd threw it back, inspired by the invention of the man on the platform.

A narrow lane to the platform had been left between the crowds of people on both sides of the street. As the correspondents appeared under the arches, young men in neat clothes with triangular badges pinned to their shirts came down the lane. They were smiling. "You are journalists?" they asked. "Yes? From which country?"

"United Press International," said one, coming down hard and equivocally on the "International."

"American," another added.

"Canadian," said a third.

"American? Canadian? Yes? You are welcome. Please, come this way. We have made a place for you on the platform where you can see everything."

As the correspondents were being led into the crowd,

one explained that the young men were cadres of the Arab Socialist Union, the only political party permitted in Egypt. The reception given the press was evidently part of a controlled mood being ordered and orchestrated from above. The Nasser government is aware of what the mobs of Cairo are capable of doing once they get out of control. The coup which brought the officers to power in 1952 was probably delayed some months by Black Saturday in January of that year. British troops in the canal zone had surrounded a police station in Ismailia and killed forty-three of its occupants in response to guerrilla attacks on them. In response to *that,* a mob burned half of Cairo (including Shepheard's Hotel), murdered scores of foreigners and looted shops while the police of King Farouk's sordid monarchy stood around and watched. In the early summer of 1967 the Egyptian government was keeping the hatreds it inspired impersonal; it did not want foreigners in Cairo doused with petrol and set afire, ripped to pieces or defenestrated. As the correspondents were marched toward the platform, the people in the crowd looked at them with dispassionate curiosity; the new arrivals were obviously foreigners and—because they were being escorted—probably living examples of the detestable, Israeli-protecting imperialism that was being denounced from the platform. But rules are rules, and the rules were intuitively sensed if not spelled out in simple language.

Television crews were jammed up against the platform behind lines of uniformed cadres who kept back the denser, standing ranks of the crowd. Above them, speaking over a steel garden of microphones, the agitator sweated and scowled out into the darkening street. He was a fat-faced man with a little mustache, enormous eyebrows and crisp black hair which glittered with oily radiance in the rays of the floodlights. Perspiration streamed from his temples and forehead and ran into the open collar of his green sport shirt as he shouted his slogans and then listened angrily to the tumult of response roaring back. Behind him all sorts of people were packed beneath the platform's carpeted ceiling— sweating cadres, a pretty, overweight popular singer, another fat person who was apparently a well-known movie star, the wives of government officials and a group of reporters who had arrived earlier.

On the carpeted back wall of the platform, two huge cartoons reminded everyone of what the rally was all about; one showed a muscular arm dangling a scrawny, squalling Jew over water—"We will push the Jews into the sea"—and the other portrayed a splendid Egyptian soldier miles high straddling the Gulf of Aqaba, with one paratrooper boot planted on Saudi Arabia and the other on the Sinai.

The new arrivals were half-hoisted up onto the platform, chairs were brought for them and they were told that the high moment would come when Achmed Shukairy, the chairman of the Palestine Liberation Organization, appeared to make a speech. Shukairy is a migratory figure in the councils of Arab extremism who has been, among other things, ambassador for both Syria and Saudi Arabia at the United Nations. In the early summer of 1967 his capacity for hellfire oratory was serving a particular purpose of the Egyptian government; since they were operating in both the intemperate world of Arab politics and the broader sphere of international diplomacy where language is supposed to mean what it says, no more, no less, the Egyptians employed Shukairy to make the utterly demented speeches that they didn't care to make themselves.

The agitator finally quit his responsive shouting with

the crowd and moved back to mop himself with a hand-kerchief. The volume of the martial music soared—including the record's scratchy defects—and curdled the hot evening air with its blasting shriek until the movie star moved up to the microphones with a bit of paper in his hand. Applause broke out on the platform (the crowd was making so much noise that it was impossible to tell if there was an extra ovation from that quarter) and people nearby pounded the actor on the back as if he were about to perform the final demolition of Israel instead of make a speech.

The music was cranked down and the oratory began again. The movie star spoke in short bursts: "Today our soldiers are stationed in the trenches ready for a great and triumphant liberation war"; "we welcome the battle that we have yearned for years to make against the usurpers of Palestine"; "oh, how glorious will be the war of revenge" and so forth. As bits of it were trans-lated by the Arab Socialist Union cadres on the plat-form, the speech sounded faintly preposterous—it would have been preposterous even had the Arabs won the last two wars. But it had a passion-harvesting effect on the crowd that stretched down the street in two blocks of living mesmerism; amid all the din the correspond-ents on the platform could see arms waving and mouths shouting. The camera crew in front of the platform turned their spotlights on the actor. His swarthy, aqui-line features became histrionically animated. He bulged his eyes, scattered spraylets of sweat from his shaking head and worked his mouth like a soft rubber ring as a thick, rich torrent of cinema Arabic gushed from him. The spotlights switched to the crowd just in front of the platform. Like a rank of grain bending before a sudden wind, the bodies surged forward and the shouting turned to screams. The uniformed cadres flung themselves against the clawing, swaying mass, and the shrieking men tried to retreat. But they couldn't because the people behind them had also been detonated by the oratory and by the glaring attention of the spotlight. Placards were hoisted. Like the rise of wounded limbs, blood-red banners came up unfurled. The Palestine Liberation Army's crude skull-and-crossbones waved back and forth in the cacophonous mélange of the actor's igniting peal and the howl of ten thousand inflamed men and children.

On the rooftops, boys danced excitedly and a woman in a long red dress grinned down at the aroused, churning mob, her hands on her hips. "The angel of death," someone muttered.

Then it was the turn of the pop singer. The trumpet of a four-piece band tootled and began to play a thumping, exciting air. The heavy singer, her smile made expressionless by dark glasses, fought her way to the microphone and began to chant in a strong, controlled voice, "Oh, how brave are our heroes! Oh, how glorious are our invincible heroes!" (Two hundred new patriotic songs had been written in Cairo that week. Their composers were officially regarded as heroes themselves.) The death's-head banners slashed back and forth, the placards jiggled and a boy in a stained shirt was flung up onto the shoulders of the crowd before the platform. People standing around the pop singer began to stamp and sway in time to the rhythm of her song. The timbers groaned and the whole platform appeared to be sagging to one side.

The boy on the shoulders of the front rank looked as if he would burst. His mouth and eyes were wide open.

"We are going to war!" cried the singer. "Oh, we are going to war, to war!"

The boy flung out his hands and squeezed his eyes

shut in an expression of joy too delirious to demonstrate. "We are going to war!" he screamed.

"Nasser!" bellowed the men who held him.

"Nasser! Nasser!"

In the general euphoric excitement that followed Israel's astonishing victory in the third Arab-Israeli war, one Western commentator with a greater talent for righteous indignation than for insight tried to explain away the Arabs and their leaders as universal psychopaths. This is equivalent to analyzing a wound as something that produces blood. God has afflicted cultures with countless plagues and deficiencies, but he has never created a race of madmen. The government that prevailed in Cairo the week before the war was not mad. It was not even extreme by Western standards. It was a government of technicians dominated by a super-Arab —super in the faults, virtues and chemistry of being that make the Arabs the people they are.

"Nasser," said one Western diplomat that week, "is a completely self-confident man. At the same time, he is a repository of all the humiliation, grievance, shame and outrage that the Arabs have acquired in a thousand years of bitter history. His mission in life is to make up for everything." Another diplomat now resident in the United States, a man who knew Nasser well through years of official dealings with him, described the President of Egypt as sane, balanced, witty and rational in private. But at the same time, he adds, Nasser becomes someone else in front of public audiences; he says things that are utterly senseless in terms of his own interests. (This is more than momentary compulsion. Nasser usually prepares his public speeches very carefully.) All of this latter analysis explains Nasser's dichotomic standing in the world. Viewed as an object rather than as an intimate human being, Nasser is either adored or detested. Most Westerners who discuss the President of Egypt from personal experience see in him many European virtues. The Arab masses see another set of virtues in their Egyptian hero—to them, his defiance and charisma seem to be an assertion of the Arab character in a world that has spent the last few centuries trampling all over that character. Thus, that which is Nasserian virtue to the Arab masses is demagoguery to Westerners, and that which is Nasserian virtue to Europeans—the evidences of reason and restraint—is weakness to the radical idealists of the Arab world.

Although he was a poor student who managed to get through only a few years of primary and secondary school—he also had an indifferent and brief bout with law after being rejected by the military college on his first try—Nasser is obviously highly intelligent and he is also widely read. He has studied the important eighteenth-, nineteenth- and twentieth-century works of Egyptian social philosophy and has read Voltaire, Montaigne, Mill and the memoirs of Chaim Weizmann. He follows the British press (and says he is amused by the virulent caricatures of himself printed in the *Daily Express*), has an airmail subscription to *Foreign Affairs* and likes to study petroleum reports put out by the University of Chicago.

There are a few literary works attributed to Nasser, the principal one being *The Philosophy of the Revolution,* which was probably written by Mohammed Heissenin Heikel, the editor and columnist of the newspaper *Al Ahram,* whose quasi-official utterances are usually taken as coming from the horse's mouth. Whoever actually put it on paper, *The Philosophy* is what Nasser wants the world to know about his thinking. Its famous passage on the three great circles reaching out from

Cairo—Arab nationalism, African liberation and Islam —is more useful to Egypt's enemies and worshippers than it is to serious analysis; like the Bible, the collected works of Lenin and New Math, the bit about the three circles can prove anything you want it to prove. That and Nasser's comparison of Egypt with Pirandello's *Six Characters in Search of an Author* (which he misquotes as "Six Personalities in Search of Actors")—the nation that fulfills a waiting role—is the usual posturing of a political hero's chapbook.

Of greater interest are Nasser's public revelations about violence. He is against it and goes to considerable lengths to say that he is against it. He describes his experiences as the youthful member of an assassination squad which gunned down an unnamed victim one evening in Cairo. Nasser tells us that he went home and lay awake all night tormented by remorse and discovered with immense relief the next morning that the victim was going to live. (Actually, the incident appears to have taken place just before the revolution when Nasser was a grown man, and the victim was a royalist general.) It is interesting, to say the least, that Nasser would put such views to the Arab world, where violence is at least a verbal and often a physical way of life. There is some historic evidence to support Nasser's claim that he hates violence. He saved the life of Farouk, the fat, dirty-minded descendant of an Albanian mercenary who was the last King of Egypt. After the revolution of 1952 a majority of the Free Officers who had engineered the coup wanted to kill Farouk. Nasser argued successfully for sending the wretched King into exile.

To repeat, everything in the Arab world exists on two levels at least. So does everything in Nasser; this is the principal feature of his super-Arabism. A revolutionary from childhood, when his uncle was arrested and imprisoned for anti-British activities, he underwent the Arab's natural temptation to violent solutions for Egypt's problems before the revolution. In *The Philosophy* he says, "I had within me a feeling of distraction which was a mixture of complex and intermingling factors; of patriotism, religion, compassion, cruelty, faith, suspicion, knowledge and ignorance." It is one of the best summaries of the elements of the Arab character ever written.

Of equal interest is the President's discussion of his disappointment immediately after the revolution when he discovered that the masses of Egypt, whom he thought he had liberated so that they could help themselves, were really not liberated at all. "After July twenty-third I was shocked by the reality. The vanguard performed its task; it stormed the walls of the fort of tyranny; it forced Farouk to abdicate and stood by expecting the mass formations to arrive at their ultimate object. It waited and waited. Endless crowds showed up, but how different is the reality from the vision! The multitudes that arrived were dispersed followers and contrasted remnants." He went, he says, to the intellectuals, politicians and theorists to see what was to be done. "Every leader we came to wanted to assassinate his rival. Every idea we found aimed at the destruction of another. If we were to carry out all that we heard, then there would not be one leader left alive."

Whether all of this is true or accurate or honestly put is not so important as the fact that this is what Nasser wants—in this case—Arab masses and Arab intellectuals to know about his opinions of them after the 1952 revolution.

As the child of the immediate confrontation, Nasser's original revolutionary impulse was directed against Britain, which, in his youth, was in the autumn of its seventy-five years of control of Egypt. Historically as well as immediately, he was bitter about the British. His book swarms with the classic Arab protest against the Balfour Declaration. In November 1917 Lord Balfour wrote a letter to Lord Rothschild which stipulated that the British were willing to turn their mandate, Palestine, over to the Jews for a National Homeland providing there was no prejudice to the non-Jewish communities living there—which meant the Arab residents of the area. (In 1923 Lord Grey asked the House of Commons how it was possible to create a National Jewish Home in Palestine without creating, at the same time, a Zionist government and thereby prejudicing the civil rights of ninety percent of the population. There were 600,000 Arabs in Palestine in 1917 and 65,000 Jews.) The Balfour Declaration contradicted earlier policy. Britain, which had wanted Arab support against Germany's ally Turkey, had made other promises concerning Palestine in the McMahon letters to Sharif Hussein of Mecca.

To Nasser, Israel originally appeared on the scene as an extension of British perfidy and British imperialism. ". . . even Israel itself was but one of the outcomes of imperialism," he says in *The Philosophy*. "If it had not fallen under British mandate, Zionism could not have found the necessary support to realize the idea of a national home in Palestine." There is no good reason to hate another nation wholesale and without qualification. But Nasser's reason, if not good, is at least consistent with his whole life and more specific than the venomous drivel put out by many other Arab leaders.

Whether Nasser is a complete prisoner of his feelings about Israel and whether he is committed permanently to Israel's physical destruction are key questions, and there are no clear answers to them. Several times he has outlined to visitors from the West an alternative solution to the whole question. Israel's natural future lies, he has said, in her Arab population—at present about ten percent of the Israeli whole. Through breeding and re-immigration these Arabs will increase over the generations until they exercise a power equivalent to that of the Jews. At that point Israel will become a bi-religious state along the lines of Lebanon (which is half Sunni Moslem and half Maronite Christian) and take some sort of place in the permanent life of the Middle East.

This theory is full of evident flaws and questionable assumptions, and whether Nasser believes in it or even believes in it some of the time is something that only God and Nasser know.

Reality is not only what exists but also what men think exists. To the Arab masses Israel is an offense that can be rectified only by its total eradication. The Arabs in general have become so obsessed with Israel that they seem to believe that all contemporary problems as well as all the grievances of history will be resolved when the Jews are pushed into the sea. The Arabs who used to live in Israel—now called the Palestinian refugees— are the symbol of the outrage. They squat in miserable camps, for the most part, where idleness gives a full-time status to the Arab capacity for hatred. The refugees have multiplied to 1,300,000 since their own diaspora began in 1948. Although many of them are highly skilled—British education—and work as technicians and teachers throughout the Middle East, the majority are idle and doomed to lives of idleness. Their poverty is desperate and their mental state cannot be explained simply by some quirk of Arab madness; living almost within sight of their lost homeland, they suffer the classic miseries of all refugees—the almost indefinable fury of one sequestered from the familiar, a hypertrophe of childhood memory, the abusing sense of being a stranger in someone else's land and at the mercy of the host. The host hasn't been very charitable—a gritty bit of evidence that the refugees are being used to postulate the case against Israel rather than symbolize it. Only Jordan has offered them full citizenship. Libya betrayed the real status of the refugees when she refused to give them citizenship because their absorption into the rest of the Arab world would dull the holy cause against Israel.

If Arab nationalism were a spiritual fact lacking only a geographic manifestation, as the Arabs like to believe, then the refugees could be absorbed into the rest of the Arab world with no real sense of alienation after a generation or two. This would not solve the problems of compensation for lost property, but it would eradicate the terrible limbo of placelessness in which the refugees presently exist and the feelings of outraged nostalgia to which their children are being bred in an endless perpetuation of the problem.

The refugees cry out to Gamel Abdul Nasser to deliver them from perdition. The cry is picked up across the whole Arab world and generalized into total protest against lost glory and present misery, with Israel as its immediate target.

The Arab world thus becomes Eliot's old man in a dry month and Nasser is the boy who reads to the old man while they wait for rain.

My house is a decayed house,
And the jew squats on the window sill, the owner,
Spawned in some estaminet of Antwerp,
Blistered in Brussels, patched and peeled in London.

He reads one book in public and yet all the evidence indicates that Nasser knows that this is not the best liturgy for the Arabs to hear. Their mobs are dispersed followers and their politicians want to murder each other. In the week before the war Nasser said that the battle would be a general one with the eradication of Israel as its objective. In the council of Arab leadership he had urged caution against Israel. In private he had suggested the formula for a peaceful solution. To La Pira, the peace-seeking mayor of Florence, Nasser confessed that he couldn't force peace with Israel on the Arab world even if he wanted to, but that he was always interested in hearing Israeli offers on the refugee problem and other questions.

He admits to a certain helplessness. We who are not powerful often take the deluded view of power that it is supreme, that it can do whatever it wants to do. The mightiest tyrants of history who fell did so because they ignored other opinions around them. This was the practical fate of Jan Kott's guilty kings.

Nasser was born with the germ of genius inside him. But his sort of genius—the genius of a leader—does not exist in a vacuum. It must be exercised, and its raw material is found among those who are willing to follow the leader. The followers, by their nature and previous history, impose limitations. The exercise of the leader is to see how far he can go in surmounting the nature and history of his followers in order to accomplish given ends. He has already defined the ends. Subsequent history will judge him on two counts: whether the ends were good and whether the leader's genius was great enough to permit him to overcome all obstacles and reach his destination.

Many of the ends of the Egyptian revolution were good. Birth control was begun, the High Aswan Dam conceived and executed, women were emancipated from the romantic status of chattels, political extremism—in the form of the communist party and the Moslem

Brotherhood—was banished, land reform was attempted and the frustrated Arab struggle with the impossibilities of Arab nationalism was softened by Nasser's abjuration of "unity of ends before unity of ranks." By the early summer of 1967, however, many things had gone wrong. The foolish war in the Yemen—originally an impulse of Arab socialism to help a republican revolt succeed against Arab royalism—was a completely useless expense of men and money; the Egyptian government's long-term debts amounted to a billion dollars and it was fighting—and losing—a financial rear-guard action against the accumulation of $250,000,000 in short-term notes. Low-cost grain shipments from the United States had been cut off, largely because of the effect on Capitol Hill in Washington of Nasser's self-defeating speeches; in its luxuriously simple view of the world, the U.S. Congress sometimes forgets to seek beneath the noise that leaders make for the reasons why they make it; Congress still considers that American aid should be a sort of reward of sweets to the good guys of this world. Nasser, clearly, had got himself out of that category. A deal for food at much severer terms hung fire for many months while the State Department and the Johnson administration struggled with Congress. Nasser finally told the United States he didn't want their food and turned to the Soviet Union.

The Egyptian government had created the mess it was in, but obviously did not intend the mess as an end. It had assembled a cabinet of technocrats to try to deal with the situation. The Prime Minister, Mohammed Sidki Sulayman, had been minister for High Dam affairs. One deputy premier, Mahmoud Yunis, was the man who had made the Suez Canal run efficiently after the Egyptians seized it in 1956. Zakariya Moheiddin, an old Nasser colleague, was a Vice President, a practical

realist who was suspicious of the ersatz socialism practiced in Egypt and who favored co-operation with the
West. Moheiddin was to play an interesting but frustrated role in the crisis before the war broke out, and he
was the man to whom Nasser proposed to give the presidency in his theatrical gesture of resignation after the
war ended.

The farthest left of Nasser's ministers in the summer
of 1967 was Ali Sabry, a former premier who had been
made the Egyptian equivalent of minister of works. The
word around Cairo was that Ali Sabry no longer was
trusted by Nasser and that he was slipping. Even *his*
leftist instinct made more obeisance to Harold Laski
than it did to Karl Marx.

There is, in other words, an indication that Nasser
was trying to clear up the mess in the period before the
crisis blew up. This was not the result of an inspired
baptism in the faith of conservative economic theory.
All the powers that could assist him—the Soviet Union,
the United States and the International Monetary Fund,
where the Egyptians were trying to stall off payments on
an old loan and get a new one—had demanded extensive
reform and revision in Egypt.

The obstacles before Nasser were not only the nature
and history of the Arabs but also the continuum of
physical misery and frustration that perpetuate the inflammable nature itself. Nasser was idolized in the burning wilderness of Arab humanity because the mission of
his charisma—to rectify all the grievances and shame of
history—was recognized even if it had never been
demonstrated.

In the process of coming to terms with his followers,
the leader must not lose them. The technique of aligning
their nature with his ends is to give the appearance of
accommodating the desires of the followers. It was in

the application of this delicate principle that Nasser failed.

He has been called the Attaturk of Egypt. But he is not. Attaturk brought the history of Turkey to an end and began a new history—one that was based on a new logic and a new set of assumptions. His genius manifested itself in a capacity to lead his people into this new history and persuade them to adjust to its logic.

Nasser's genius is not ultimate, just as his power is not supreme. At crucial moments he succumbs to the desires of his followers and they—for those moments—become the leaders while he assumes the role of solitary follower.

Upon being warned by the Soviet embassy that Israel was planning an attack on Syria, Nasser moved his troops into the desert. The charge was upon him that he had hidden too long behind the United Nations Emergency Force that barricaded the hostilities of Egypt and Israel. Nasser demanded the force's removal and U Thant—perhaps to Nasser's astonishment—complied, thus quickening the momentum of events. The vast gallery of the Arab world cheered the hero moving toward the destiny they had always demanded of him. As the spectator's excitement is aroused, action creates an appetite for action, and this conveys itself to the actor in the drama. The gallery called for victory, and the proceeding hero—wary of war and yet knowing that oratory would no longer be enough—swerved on his course and seized Sharm El Sheik, which commanded the Gulf of Aqaba.

The followers had become the leader and he had become the uncontrolled follower, and the third mystery of the crisis had accomplished itself.

Foreign observers, no matter how detached, are always somewhat susceptible to the atmosphere of the capital in which they are doing their observing. No one can be totally immune to his surroundings, and this was true of the journalists and diplomats in Cairo during the week of May 28 to June 2, 1967. The Nasser government, unaware of the full implications of blocking the Gulf of Aqaba, did not intend to go to war and didn't think there would be a war. It was counting on a victory rising out of gestures that were verbally but not physically opposed. On its side, the Egyptian government knew the difference and it was operating on the assumption that the Israelis would adhere to the difference. If, on the other hand, there *was* to be a war, the Egyptians, if they thought about it at all at that euphoric stage, probably thought they had, in the abstract, a chance to win. The Arab mind, in refuge from its history, also blurs history to soften its pain. The Arab defeat in the 1948 Israeli War of Independence was the result of imperialist machinations, and 1956 was considered a victory in Cairo—probably because the Egyptians had managed to hold on to the Suez Canal when it was all over. These judgments made the score of past wars with the Israelis look at least even, and if war was to come again, fortune might well bend to the Arabs. Their curiously incomplete military planning for a 1967 war was based upon the presumption of a conflict lasting from two to three weeks.

To one degree or another, the correspondents and diplomats who gathered at Jean-Pierre Guyot's house on Monday evening shared a good many of these assumptions. There were about twenty men and women at the French attaché's flat on El Saleh Ayoub Street: a French-speaking West German diplomat; several correspondents from the Nile Hilton contingent; the Yugoslavian Moslem; the *Le Monde* man who knew everybody in Cairo;

the bureau chief of Agence France-Presse. The French correspondents brought their wives; the families of the American journalists resident in Cairo had been evacuated with the U.S. embassy dependents. There were no American diplomats at Guyot's. They seemed to have gone to earth in a burrow of embarrassment and uncertainty.

Over Mme Guyot's excellent buffet the opinion was offered for the hundredth time that if war broke out the Israelis would start it, not the Egyptians. At that point Nasser's achievements looked very impressive. By the moves he had taken to date he had reasserted his supremacy in the Middle East as the only author of historic movement, completed the "return to conditions as they were before 1956" by pushing the United Nations out of the Sinai Desert, Sharm El Sheik and the Gaza Strip and also, at the same time, abolished the charge that he was cowering behind the skirts of the United Nations. The socialist President of Egypt had forced a pace upon his royal Arab opponents, making them vassals to his policy. (The Saudi Radio at Jidda had been saying that the time had come to "bury differences over the Yemen" and unite in the struggle against Israel.) Nasser had also—he thought—derailed an imagined Israeli plan to attack Syria and he had demonstrated that his maddening brothers in Damascus had no secure life in the Middle East without Egyptian protection. (The 1958–1961 period of single-state partnership between Egypt and Syria had ended with an abrasive withdrawal by the Syrians, who had asked Nasser to be their president in the first place. Nasser had later called this experiment "three and a half years of endless troubles." He said that he had had to spend so much time on the messy affairs of the Syrians that he hadn't had much opportunity to administer Egypt.)

All of this, as seen from Cairo, created the logic that the Egyptians had nothing to gain and quite possibly everything to lose by starting a war. In addition, a well-known Israeli principle of Middle Eastern life seemed to stand as a barricade between the existent situation and war. The Israelis had always presumed that the inability of the Arabs to unite in common purpose was a great safety factor in the Middle East. Though Nasser had taken the verbal play away from the Arab monarchies, there had as yet been no move toward practical consolidation for the purposes of war by the royal Arabs and the radical Arabs. A few symbolic gestures had been made: Kuwaiti forces were coming into Egypt, and the Iraqis had sent contingents to Jordan and Syria (thereby triggering another uprising by the gleeful Kurds, who knew the deployment of all forces in Iraq).

These gestures of military co-ordination, plus others that had been more or less promised, would not seem significant to the Israelis, the foreign observers in Cairo thought. The state of relations between the three principal belligerent states that surrounded Israel was not promising from the Arab point of view. Syria and Jordan weren't speaking to each other (a few days earlier the Syrian foreign minister, Dr. Ibrahim Makhus, had referred to Palestinian refugees "suffering in the prisons of reaction on the West Bank of the Jordan") and Achmed Shukairy, the Palestine Liberation Organization chairman, had used Cairo Radio—doubtless with Cairo's blessing—to denounce "the reactionary Arab leaders in Jordan, Saudi Arabia and Tunisia"; this, from Israel's point of view, was a nice, healthy affirmation that Egypt still looked upon King Hussein of Jordan as a maggot in the apple of life.

The day after Guyot's dinner party one of the key pieces in the balanced structure of Middle Eastern tensions moved. King Hussein flew into Cairo and signed a five-year mutual-defense agreement with President Nasser. The structure rumbled and slipped a little, and suddenly war was much closer.

The Hashemite Kingdom of Jordan is, like Belgium, an invention of that hundred-year period when British diplomacy was restlessly rearranging the map of various parts of the world. Jordan was founded on the Arabs of the upper Arabian peninsula in the relatively tranquil days when the Palestinian Arabs were still living in Palestine. There is a ferocious decency about the Bedouins of the desert as compared to the equally ferocious but Byzantine mentality of the coastal Arabs. God, in the desert, is the creator of the law and the world; in Cairo and Baghdad, God is a political figure who went to the London School of Economics and has been partly transformed from an omnipotent author of inexplicable destiny into a protective phantom who approves of whatever the Arabs happen to be planning at any given moment. God has been officially exiled from Damascus. When King Hussein speaks of God, he is apparently sincere.

This native theocratic decency had put the Hashemite house in a tormenting bind. Of all the surrounding Arab states, Jordan shared the longest border with Israel. If this were the best of all possible worlds (a proposition impossible even to consider in the Middle East), the kings of Jordan would probably just as soon recognize Israel as an inevitable fact of life and get on with the rest of living. Hussein's beloved grandfather, Abdullah, went so far as to operate on that principle. After Israel came into being, Abdullah negotiated secretly with its government, whose agents used to come to his summer palace near Jericho to talk to the old King about a modus vivendi between Jordan and the new Jewish state. This streak of reason cost Abdullah his life. He was gunned down by a Palestinian refugee as he left a mosque in Jerusalem a few years later. Jordan had taken in hundreds of thousands of the Arab refugees from Israel, and the irony of the means by which his grandfather came to die must have occurred to Hussein as Abdullah expired in his arms.

Perhaps unfortunately for himself, King Hussein was not an ironist by nature. Fortunately for them, the Palestinian refugees continued to enjoy the benefits of Jordanian hospitality under Hussein. Jobs were found for a good many of them, they were offered citizenship, and thousands took up residence on the West Bank, that double bulge of Jordan that protruded into Israel on the western side of the Jordan River. Thousands more languished in Jordanian camps.

Hussein, if an instinctively decent young man, was not a subtle one. A Western diplomat stationed in Amman who knew Hussein well said that the young King had a fighter pilot's mentality—everything was either up or down, black or white. The attempts on his life by Palestinian refugees and agents of radical Arab governments are beyond cataloguing. Amman sometimes gave the impression of being a stage set for a lurid game of hide-and-seek between Hussein and his would-be assassins. There was in the King's personality something that came close to the death-wish phenomenon. He seemed to get an inordinate pleasure out of the process of surviving. He was fond of driving around his dusty capital in a well-known automobile, and when he was not playing lethal games with his enemies Hussein enjoyed such potential blood sports as sky-diving, flying, scuba diving and going too fast in sports cars. All of this drove his Circassian bodyguards to distraction.

The King also had a patriarchal impulse which is rare

in men so young (he was thirty-one at the time of the 1967 crisis and had spent fourteen exhilaratingly dangerous years on the throne of Jordan). Speaking excellent, r-rolling English, he was fond of talking about "the Jordanian family" and sometimes he referred to the population as his children; Hussein was mad about all things military and his troops were always "my brothers."

This sense of the patriarchic created in King Hussein a perpetual feeling of sorrow at the divisions in his Jordanian family. He was probably unable to understand the depths of resentment in the Palestinian refugees, who demand leadership which expresses itself in passion equivalent to theirs and which promises action violent enough to salve their rage. With the sensitivity of the truly obsessed, the refugees whiffed Hussein's temperance and this made them hate him to a degree that pushed aside any feelings of gratitude they may have had for Jordan's kindness to them. The mission of the refugees, bloated and carnal though it may have been, was to reclaim Palestine, not accommodate themselves to their present surroundings. The temperature of their obsession rose as the Middle Eastern crisis mounted, and this, finally, was the pressure that drove Hussein to Cairo.

At a press conference in the Egyptian capital that followed the signing of the mutual-defense agreement Hussein sat between Shukairy and Nasser, smiling with the forced amiability of one who has just swallowed a bad oyster at an archbishop's luncheon table, knows it, but can't do anything about it. Shukairy, a squat, white-haired man, wore the contemplative expression of a sow about to give birth as Nasser told the watching reporters that he and Hussein had forgotten the differences between them because "We face challenges, not only Israel's challenge but also those of its supporters—

America and Britain." The Jordanian and Egyptian military establishments were "on the front line as one man" (under the five-year agreement, Hussein agreed to the extraordinary proposition that a general of Egypt's unexceptional army would command the first-rate forces of Jordan's Arab Legion) and the President of Egypt wanted to thank his "dear brother" and to wish "the fraternal Jordanian people every glory and success."

From the Israeli point of view, the situation had suddenly deteriorated. The new unity implied a much more coherent Arab plan of attack on Israel. True, Syria was not in total harmony with either Egypt or Jordan. The guerrilla-minded strategists of Damascus put their faith in a long Viet-Congish war of attrition against Israel, the sort of war their El Assifa terrorists had already begun. The Syrians were uneasy about direct all-out confrontations with the enemy even though their Soviet advisers had been training them in the techniques of conventional warfare for years. As for Syrian relations with Jordan, the Hussein-Nasser pact changed nothing in the bitter revolutionary minds of Damascus. They were seeing things in a grander context as the Syrian radio went on the air the next morning. The coming battle would end "only after the destruction of the Zionist base and the overthrow of the rule of Hussein, Feisal and Bourguiba and all imperialist and Zionist lackeys and the establishment of a unified socialist Arab society."

Still, General Fawzi had managed to co-ordinate Syria into the over-all Egyptian plan—Syria could hardly refuse to do her part even though she had grave misgivings about the sort of war being prepared for. She was also committed under a Damascus-Cairo mutual-defense pact. Quixotically, the Syrians never *did* do their part when the final squeeze was on.

Perhaps because the Egyptians never, in the final analysis, believed that war would actually come, their plan was only half drawn. Or perhaps they believed that someone or other would step in and stop things before Israel was totally annihilated. The Arab plans were odd in another respect: they never defined exactly how the war would start if—again—it ever came.

The campaign was to begin with the simultaneous activation of three and a half armies on four fronts (the two Iraqi brigades in Jordan, the Kuwaitis and Shukairy's Palestine Liberation irregulars did not really constitute a fourth army) and a heavy bombing campaign. The bombing was crucial, especially in the big battle for the Negev Desert in southern Israel. There were seven Egyptian divisions in the Sinai, three of them lined up in offensive forward position near the coastal fortress of El Arish. Their task was to roll into the Gaza Strip, join up with Shukairy's refugee forces and then split, one part heading north into coastal Israel while the other part fought south into the Negev toward Beersheba, the principal Israeli desert city. Meanwhile, between 200 and 300 tanks faced Kuntilla on the eastern end of the central Sinai. Their assignment was to shoot their way up the main Negev road through Nitzana and head for the Jordanian border—to cut the Negev in two—and form a second arm of the Arab pincer closing in on Beersheba. A Jordanian force beefed up with Egyptian commandos was supposed to head for Beersheba from Sammua in the southern part of the Jordanian West Bank.

While all of this was going on in the south, Jordanian and Iraqi forces were to break into Israel from Tulkarm on the West Bank and march nine miles across the narrowest part to Natanya on the seacoast, this cutting the country in two at its center. In the north, the Syrians were supposed to swoop down from the Heights of Golan onto the Israeli plain, take Haifa and Nazareth and other cities in the area. It was hoped that the Syrians would have Lebanese help. (Co-ordination with Lebanon was pretty hazy.) Syrian plans assumed that the plain could be reached and Haifa occupied in five days. The called-for advance was at the rate of twenty to twenty-five kilometers a day and the whole operation from start to finish would take six days. If the Egyptians took Beersheba and then rushed down upon Eilat at the end of the Negev and at the head of the Gulf of Aqaba, it was imperative that the Syrians put on a ferocious drive in the north.

And bombing. From four air bases in the Sinai the MIG's, Sukhois and TU-16's would come in waves, rocketing and bombing Israeli airfields, Hawk missile sites, the Eilat airdrome, broadcasting station and oil storage depot. From the El Arish field, for example, the Second Air Brigade would blast army camps, oil storage depots in central Israel, pumping stations, radar stations and electrical stations. Saturation bombing was crucial to the whole operation.

The Jordanians would carry the brunt of the ground war in the centrally populated regions of Israel. In the headquarters of the Hashemite Brigade near Ramallah a series of plans had been drawn up for operations against Israeli settlements. Most of the raids on the settlements were worked out on a three-company basis: one company to break into the settlement and kill all of its inhabitants, the second to stand by and rescue the first if it got into trouble and the third company to keep help from coming for the attacked settlers.

All of these plans were worked out to the point of a deep penetration of Israel on the four fronts. Then they stopped. The final stage does not appear to have been worked out. Only the Jordanians understood that it was imperative that everybody be killed, as otherwise the invading armies would be harassed by Israeli guerrillas. How the Arabs planned to pacify what was left of the cities after the saturation bombing was not specified.

If anything went wrong, the Egyptians had a second massive army backed up in the hills of the western Sinai Desert on either side of the Mitla Pass. This second line of defense, only twenty miles from the Suez Canal, was the legacy of Soviet strategy in its arrangement.

However crude and incomplete, the Arab plan demonstrated to Israeli intelligence that the Arabs had at least given serious thought to the possibilities of fighting. But the full military potential of the situation was not visible to the diplomats and journalists in Cairo. Toward the middle of the week the U.S. aircraft carrier *Intrepid* came through the Suez Canal and reporters were allowed to go out and see it. They crossed a bit of desert which revealed nothing of the Egyptian Sinai deployment and arrived at 2:00 a.m. at Port Said, the city at the head of the canal which used to enjoy a reputation as the dirty-postcard capital of the world. At dawn the *Intrepid* moved through the canal. The Egyptian press later printed stories of massive demonstrations on the banks of the canal, but all the correspondents saw as they followed the carrier down to Ismailia was a few Egyptians waving their shoes at the big, gray American presence.

Throughout the rest of the week, absurdity, enigma and nastiness came together to create a creeping sense of stagnation upon the brink. The banners draped across Cairo's heat-baked boulevards increased in number and ferocity each day. One morning the correspondents saw two marionettes hanging side by side with nooses around their necks. One was President Johnson and the other was a dark, hawk-nosed Jew with the Star of David upon his cap. With the same stridency that it used in denouncing the evil machinations of imperialism and the mortal affront of Israel's being, the Egyptian press announced that henceforth James Bond films and American westerns would be banned in Cairo because they portrayed white Europeans in the role of invincible heroes triumphing over the animals and people of Africa.

The government remained invisible, its mood and intention impossible to gauge from its public utterances. The pronouncements of Cairo had begun to take on the deafening monotony of a pop song played over and over again; the words originally had some meaning, but they had been worn out of all definition by repetition. Anything that deviated from the general line of denunciation and righteousness glimmered like a sapphire in sludge. One morning the English-language *Egyptian Gazette* appeared on the breakfast tables of the Nile Hilton with a story about the union of Egyptian customs officials, which had its headquarters in Alexandria. The union's membership had resolved to struggle with mind, heart, fingernails and life itself to keep a long list of articles and commodities from reaching the Israelis through the Gulf of Aqaba. As the reporters pored over the list, they could not find crude oil on it. The sapphire gleamed. The Gulf of Aqaba had two principal significances for Israel: it was her avenue to trade with Africa and Asia, and it was her conduit for crude oil coming up to the refinery at Eilat.

At almost the same moment that this story appeared in Cairo, an Egyptian diplomat in Washington told the State Department that the blockade of the Gulf of

Aqaba would conform to the American Battle Act. Crude oil isn't on the Battle Act embargo list either. The suspicion was born—stronger in the minds of diplomats in the West than among the correspondents in Cairo—that the Egyptians *were,* in fact, aware that they had accomplished a great deal so far and wanted to tone down the crisis a little before things got out of hand. This was one of the most interesting moments of the week before the war. In the closed annals of that moment there will lie forever an unanswered question about whether Cairo had suddenly, if briefly, grasped the fact that the closing of the Gulf of Aqaba was a final act which Israel could not and would not accept. The moment passed. On Saturday the French embassy in Egypt was told that crude oil was in fact on the list of embargoed goods.

There was another moment when Cairo gave the impression that its preachments of militancy were not beyond discussion. The Americans had been playing an intense game of time-buying in the United Nations and beyond it (so intense that they lost perspective on time). President Johnson had sent letters to the Syrian, Israeli and Egyptian governments urging caution. At the same time the United States was developing a British plan on the Aqaba question. In its first stage the plan would have had fifteen to twenty-five nations sign a declaration on the freedom of innocent passage through international waterways. In its second phase the Anglo-American scheme called for the creation of an international flotilla to open the gulf if the declaration failed to sway Nasser. London and Washington became so absorbed in the plan that time ran out on them; they were still working away at it when the war broke out.

On quite another level the British and the Americans were working triple-time to keep everyone involved as cool as possible. There was one scary moment when the United States ambassador in Tel Aviv cabled the State Department that he was losing his ability to restrain. A blizzard of telegrams poured back, and they contained, apparently, sufficient persuasions to argue the Israelis into another pause. On the Arab side, the object of the Anglo-American drill was to impress upon the Egyptians and anyone else who would listen that—in the judgment of the U.S. Joint Chiefs of Staff—the Arabs would suffer a catastrophic defeat if they got into a shooting war with the Israelis. (In this, American military intelligence was a little more realistic than its Soviet counterpart. The Russians in the Middle East apparently persuaded themselves and their masters in Moscow that, in a crunch, the Arabs could take the Israelis. This misapprehension may have risen, in part, from the natural euphoria of the Soviet military advisers about their Egyptian clients. American military advisers in Vietnam have displayed the same euphoria about the troops they have trained. There is also some question about how much the Russians really knew about the *whole* Egyptian army. The soldiers that the Soviet advisers had trained were of or above the rank of lieutenant colonel. Part of the subsequent Egyptian defeat was caused by the lamentable relations between senior and junior officers and between officers and ranks.)

The problem for the Americans in their urgings of caution upon the Arabs was to find someone to talk to. Since the U.S. embassy in Cairo had got all tangled up in its own harness, it was of no use. Washington, therefore, sent a secret emissary to see President Nasser. He was Robert Anderson, the former Secretary of the Treasury. Anderson offered to have Vice President Humphrey come to Cairo if Cairo thought that personal contact would do any good. For several months the Johnson administration had been thinking about sending Mr. Humphrey to Egypt to see if he could dampen down the Nasser government's suspicion that the United States was trying to destroy it. To Anderson, President Nasser offered, instead, to send Zakariya Moheiddin—the pro-Western Vice President, who was known to be pro-Western in Washington—to see the Americans. Moheiddin was to be accompanied by the Egyptian foreign minister and the visit was to be absolutely secret—probably to protect President Nasser from fresh charges of indecision from the Syrians and the Jordanians.

The Egyptian party was due to arrive in Washington on Wednesday, June 7. It would have been smuggled into the White House by the back door and given the American intelligence estimates of the war's outcome and any other persuasions that would have helped. Suddenly and inexplicably, on Saturday, June 3, Cairo leaked the fact of an impending Moheiddin visit. When the war broke out on June 5, rendering the visit impossible and pointless, American officials were still working on the script of what they would say to Moheiddin. Another mystery of Egypt's private view of the crisis lies buried in the foiled Moheiddin trip to Washington.

Like a tightrope walker with a broken heart, the government in Cairo kept its innermost feelings from showing as it bobbed and balanced its way toward the end of the week. Its step seemed sure enough to the reporters and diplomats who watched. The noise of propaganda, the crowds flowing in the sun and the consistency of dry, withering heat created a sense of normalcy altered only by the talk of war. Talk is the alpha and omega of the Arabs; it is often the only thing that ever happens, and to the Nile Hilton cadres it began to seem, by Thursday evening, that talk was all that *would* happen. The correspondents were beginning to get the restless feeling which precedes a realization that the matter being covered is a non-event. The mood, Guyot had said at noon, was decidedly dégonflé. Cables had gone out Thursday afternoon to news desks all over the world requesting permission to leave by the week end. Some came back ordering reporters out on Friday. Other editors suggested a stay for one more week end just for the hell of it.

A few correspondents went to one of the Hilton night clubs to watch Nahed Sabry, the belly dancer. They thought it might be a good idea to interview *her* on the crisis since there was nobody else to talk to and not much else to write about.

In the empty, carpeted night club on Thursday evening Miss Sabry went through the spastic convolutions of a decorous belly dance (the puritanical Nasser regime had decreed that the actual belly itself must be covered; though Miss Sabry skirted the law by covering her tum with yellow chiffon, the end effect was still something like watching cricket without bats) while a band of white-robed men plucked zithers, banged on little drums and clattered castanets. She whirled, stamped, contorted her body in a sort of all-in hiccup and had nothing illuminating to say about the crisis. Later a middle-aged fortune teller in a long gown and bi-focals predicted futures, tried halfheartedly to wheedle a job as a translator and then said, "I hate them Yehudis. If Nasser give me a gun I just go and kill them!" It appeared, more than ever, as if the non-event were talking itself out of existence in the sludge and stars of Cairo at midnight.

Alitalia's flight to Rome left early in the morning. Some of the departing correspondents got up a little before dawn. Cairo was switched off and lay immobilized in that gray light of pre-day that is as soft and inconclusive as a mutter. It was Friday, Cairo's last Friday of peace, and already the muezzins were in the towers calling the first hour of prayer. In the mosques that Sabbath day the mullahs would call down jihad—a holy war—upon the Jews of Israel. God would serve the cause, and the cause would make proper deference to God; a few days later Field Marshal Abad El-Hakim Amer, the deputy commander of the Egyptian armed forces, would issue his War Command Number Two, and that call to order and victory would begin with the words, "In the Name of the Merciful and Beloved God . . ."

From the minarets in the last hour before the relentless sun rose on the last Sabbath of peace, the muezzins proclaimed that God was one and Mohammed was his Messenger.

The Arabs and Islam are indivisible and Islam is the last revelation. The word of God was revealed to man in stages—through Adam, Abraham, Moses and Noah (whose son Shem gave the Jews and the Arabs the name Semite), through Aaron, Isaiah and Jesus. The races of the Middle East were created before the last word—the Jews descending from Abraham's legitimate son Isaac and the Arabs from his bastard Ishmael; "he will be a wild man," said an angel to Ishmael's mother, the Egyptian servant girl Hagar, "his hand will be against every man and every man's hand shall be against him." Then, to Ishmael's nomadic descendants the last word was given in a series of revelations to an illiterate sixth-century merchant named Mohammed. The word was given in Arabic, and Mohammed wrote it down.

Arabic, Islam and the Arabs are indivisible: each perpetually re-creates the others in an endless process of cross-pollination until words are exalted to a point where they describe their own reality. At Al-Azhar University men spend years learning to recite the books of the Koran with the proper rhythm and nuance; Islam is a religion almost devoid of theology, but it cries, proclaims, croons, chants, weeps, laughs, implores and creates in a torrential flow of changeless Arabic, a tongue whose beauty shocks the senses of even those who don't speak it. The repetitiousness of Islam withers the imagination and sometimes calcifies enlightenment, but it is gorgeous and mesmerizing to listen to in recitation. In *Mountolive* Lawrence Durrell describes a blind old Imam's night of speaking the Koranic suras:

> They waited now with emotion for that old voice, melodious and worn with age, to utter the opening strophes of the holy book, and there was nothing feigned in the adoring attention of the circle of venal faces. Some licked their lips and leaned forward eagerly, as if to take the phrases upon their lips; others lowered their heads and closed their eyes as if against a new experience in music. The old preacher sat with his waxen hands folded in his lap and uttered the first sura, full of the soft, warm coloring of a familiar understanding, his voice a little shaky at first but gathering power and assurance from the silence as he proceeded. His eyes now were as wide and lustreless as a dead hare's. His listeners followed the notation of the verses as they fell from his lips with care and rapture, gradually seeking their way together out into the main stream of the poetry like a school of fish following a leader by instinct out into the deep sea.

The holy language intoxicates and, at the same time, anesthetizes the brain so that only language comes through; language creates a four-cornered world watched over by the God of Islam complete with its heaven of cool rivers and a hell of pitch smoke and brambles, and language points the way to each. In the purer world of language everything is possible and everything will be. The heat of the desert and poverty's crawling wretchedness evaporate in the intimate thunder of the word. For fourteen hundred years the Arabs have turned inward upon this spoken world, and the brain first senses and then comes to know without doubt that there is not one reality but two, and that the one which is said is better than the one which is. A tragedy of errors had triggered the Arabs up to the threshold of war in the early summer of 1967. The words of the politicians and of the broadcasting stations had created the fervid mood that was as essential a preparation for possible combat as the battle plans of the Arabs. "We are going to war, to war!" sang the pop singer at the rally in the dusk. "We are going to war!" screamed the boy in rapture almost too delirious to bear.

Islam is a religion without an ordained priesthood. Mohammed himself was not divine, but very human indeed; he was not perfect, according to one mullah, but he lived a very good life and his ways should be imitated. The suras of the holy Koran are the revelations and the sunnas are compiled out of what people remembered about Mohammed's views on the best way to lead a daily life. Pork, along with alcohol, is forbidden, and one can have four wives at a time if capable of properly caring for them. Jesus is regarded as a prophet but mortal ("God," said the mullah, "has no sons, wives or relatives") and the Koran credits him with more miracles than the New Testament; he talked in his cradle and, as a child, made little birds of clay wihch assumed life and flew away. Those who know their way through the

Koran tend to speak of Mohammed with less awe than Christians use in talking about Jesus; the Prophet's mortality, his periodic fits of bad temper and various amatory transgressions make him unmistakably human and he is regarded with affectionate humor as well as with the respect due to the recipient of God's word.

It is said that no one can properly understand the Koran unless he knows Arabic. "Islam" means "I submit," and the God who emerges from the translated Koran is, like the God of the Jews and Christians, a being whose arbitrary character requires a good deal of submission. "God," says the Koran, "is not to be inquired of as to what he does." And the best way to accommodate oneself to the Creator's apparently capricious tendency to guide one man to glory and another to misery is to accept without human questioning. "Covet not the advantage which God has given to some over others." Islam is a religion without the lugubrious concept of original sin—Adam and Eve *did* sin, but their heirs did not inherit the consequences—and man is born pure. In a complicated concept, Moslems believe that God knows the outcome of every life, since he created the beginning and the end before the beginning began; at the same time, man is given choices and can redeem himself through virtuous practices. God knows what choice he will make, but man doesn't— hence, a sort of earthly free will under an all-knowing cosmic umbrella. Virtuous practice is outlined in Islam's five pillars of wisdom: acceptance that there is only one God and that Mohammed was his final Prophet, prayer five times a day, fasting during the holy month of Ramadan, acts of charity and making a pilgrimage to Mecca at least once in one's lifetime if it is financially possible. "Prayer leads us halfway to God, fasting to his threshold, but alms-giving to his presence."

The notion that one is, in the final analysis, subject to the will of an inexplicable God is the source of the Arab character's fatalism. A child born blind, a spavined camel or a dry well is explained and accepted as God's will more easily in Islam than in Christianity. The fatalism also facilitates the tendency of Arabs to brush aside the defeats of the immediate past and to ignore their lessons; these, too, were the will of God and maybe the next time it will be different. On June 8 a shattered King Hussein went on the radio and said, "Although the setback we have suffered is worse than expected, it is best that we submit to the will of God."

Nasser says, in *The Philosophy,* that Islam could make its adherents mighty if only they could find a way to unite under it: "a co-operation that does not deprive them of their loyalty to their countries but which guarantees for them and their brethren a limitless power." Though Egypt's revolution is strictly secular and ostensibly socialist, it goes to great lengths to accommodate Islam. It has to. Islam is one of the roots of the people upon whom Nasser is building a state. Even the proletarian Syrians don't dare trample too hard on religion. A Syrian officer said, just before the war, that Islam was passé and ought to be put in a museum; he was publicly reprimanded.

Though it fully credits Judaism as one of its sources and though Mohammed wrote the world's first constitution that accepts the freedom of conscience—the charter of Medina—Islam's utterances on the Jews are ambivalent: "Unto you your religion and unto me my religion," Mohammed is supposed to have said (he once invited some Christians to hold their services in his mosque) and, "Wilt thou then force men to believe when belief can come only from God?" But he began struggling with the Jews during the years of the Hegira in

Medina. He destroyed one Jewish tribe that he thought was plotting against him. After the Prophet's death one of the early caliphs embarked upon a campaign to drive the Jewish tribes out of the Arabian desert. "God fight the Jews and Christians!" says the Koran. "How they lie!" In the total accumulations of their misery, however, Jews probably fared better under Islam than they did under Christianity.

It is a popular notion among non-Moslems that every military campaign Moslems undertake is a holy war. Actually, the Koran is rather specific on the question of jihad; it is supposed to be fought on Arab soil and it is always in the service of God—or against his enemies. Jihad does create some special sanctions: "And if you be killed or die in God's service, this is a remission of sin and a mercy from God more precious than that which you can gather, and if you die or be killed it is always before God that you shall meet again." Those who die in a jihad are supposed to go automatically to paradise and spend the rest of eternity lolling without sin or exhaustion in the arms of dark-eyed houris.

Yet the very repetition of Islam generalizes its principles, and on Friday, June 2, jihad was being proclaimed from the mosques of Cairo. The opaque vapor of language rose to obscure whatever memories there were of the blood and iron in two other wars with Israel. In a better world of words the Arabs were invincible and victory only awaited the doing. The reality was invisible —the armies in the Sinai, the government in Cairo, the incomplete plans. In the pure, four-square world of language, everything was possible and everything would be.

For the first few hours that Friday morning a thin

cover of even gray clouds protected Cairo from the sun. A handful of sleep-numb passengers had their tickets taken in the Alitalia office on the ground floor of the Nile Hilton. They got into a bus parked under the rear entrance, where tall palm trees in pots stood in black silhouette against the sky. A heavy Egyptian man wearing a bulging suit and dark glasses got in after them and sat in the rear of the bus. He looked bored and grumpy. For some unfathomable reason, all the secret police in North Africa seem compelled to identify themselves by wearing a familiar uniform of clothes, glasses and facial expression.

Cairo was coming awake as the bus went through its streets toward the airport. Men with brown paper lunch bags under their arms were coming out of side streets. Dirty, unshaven creatures in long, brown galabias pushed wooden carts with an appearance and a weariness which implied that yesterday and today had flowed together in their labors; a pretty girl in Western dress stood waiting for a tram, her cleanliness and clothing a contrast against muddy streets and the lattice of scaffolding around a crumbling building. The morning's new banners of exhortation all featured a crude picture of the Egyptian paratrooper boot crushing a Jew and a star-spangled top hat meant to represent the United States.

Beyond the compounds of the intelligentsia on the edge of the city, the desert stretched away to low sand hills. Beyond *them* there was a streak of gleaming silver between the clouds and the horizon where the sun was trying to penetrate to its conquered world.

At the airport, flights to all parts of Europe were being called over the loudspeakers in six different languages. For those who had spent the week in Cairo the names of the cities and the images they flashed upon the mind were a cultural restorative, a reminder of another continent where words were more precise and colors brighter.

In the customs check-out hall a young official took an Anthony Powell novel from a departing traveler and flipped through its pages. "It is not dirty?"

"No."

"Oh."

As the Alitalia passengers sat in the departure lounge drinking coffee, the sun burst through the clouds and laid its terrible light upon the tarmac and the desert.

To the Arabs, victory had been achieved by the act of proclaiming it and Israel had lost its identity except as the object of Cairo's scorn and the speculation of diplomats. The time had come to see if Israel existed at all.

At last the Alitalia flight was called and the passengers filed out to the plane. The secret policeman stopped on the terrace and watched them go. He took a deep breath, yawned and fumbled at a paper cigarette pack with his thick fingers.

The Caravelle rose into the heat. The morning mist was burning off and there was a plume of dust moving in the desert to the east. Nasser had won a great victory and there was nothing visible from the Cairo perspective that would cause Israel to fight. The departing passengers had succumbed to Egypt's sequestered logic.

The aircraft crossed the dun-colored coast. Profound Mediterranean blue welcomed its passengers back to the real world.

TEL AVIV

June 4 - June 9

I am afeard there are few die well that die in a battle;
for how can they charitably dispose of any thing
when blood is their argument? Now, if these men do
not die well, it will be a black matter for the king that
led them to it, whom to disobey were against all pro-
portion of subjection.

SHAKESPEARE, *King Henry V*

NOBODY KNOWS WHO THE JEWS ARE, BUT EVERY-
body in the West thinks he knows what Israel is
—a rectification of two millennia of shame, a desert
become garden, 7,800 square miles of energetic virtue
in a world gone all fat, complicated and pointless.

It doesn't really matter that this definition is too simple; it is the definition operated on in Europe and North
America. That society spent most of its history indicting
the Jews for their imagined sins of greediness, exclusiv-
ity and Christ-murdering. It always assumed that the
Jews were guilty. Now the West seeks Jewish forgive-
ness by making acts of obeisance toward Israel. It now
assumes that the Jews of Israel and all the other Jews
in the world are one and the same people. This isn't
precisely true, either, but it is the assumption operated
on by Western gentiles, including the Honorable James
Tate, Mayor of Philadelphia.

In the summer of 1967 Mayor Tate was in a difficult
campaign for re-election. His opponent was a Jew and
it was therefore as natural as instinct that the mayor
would fly to Tel Aviv on the evening of June 4 to
check, as he said, "on former Philadelphians living in
Israel to see if they are all right." If this gesture didn't

relieve the anxieties of Jewish voters, it might at least stir their gratitude on election day.

There were plenty of reasons for anxiety. The grid of crisis was glowing so brightly that Mayor Tate's trip seemed not only pertinent but somewhat courageous. Israel was no place to be; tourists had been leaving in droves while flights of news correspondents moved in the opposite direction. These were ominous harbingers to the public, which usually judges crises by indices as simple as mathematics and a literal acceptance of whatever either belligerent says. One hundred and ten million Arabs were making blood-curdling noises in the direction of two and a half million Jews. Even if the thought *had* occurred that population statistics didn't have much to do with the real situation, the voyages and utterances of great men confirmed that the peril to Israel was grave indeed.

Powerful nations usually inflame public sensibilities by their efforts to tranquilize. On May 23 President Johnson had said that the United States was all for world order based on law and believed that it was illegal to block the Gulf of Aqaba. The first part of the statement raised the fear that the United States had decided to leave Israel's fate in the palsied hands of the United Nations. The second part sounded like—but wasn't—juridical quibbling. On the 25th of May Israel's foreign minister appeared in Washington for urgent consultations in high places. Abba Eban manages to look both shocked and grave in his public appearances, and when he turns up in Western capitals during tense periods things seem unusually bad.

Ambassador Arthur Goldberg, relieved for a moment of his role as apologist to the world for America's violent solution to the Vietnam problem, said that the United States was willing to work inside or outside the

United Nations to preserve peace—another indication
that the Americans were largely limiting their defense
of Israel to the use of rhetoric. This impression was
heightened on May 26 when the White House pleaded
with Israel to restrain herself. Washington said it was
working up a plan.

When all of this noise and assertion was placed
against the military situation in the Middle East, the
cumulative effect was enough to frighten Israel's parti-
sans into a state of distraction. Iraqi, Algerian and
Kuwaiti troops had moved onto the territory of the
Arab states immediately bordering Israel. Seven Egyptian divisions—including 900 tanks—were deployed in
forward positions across the upper Sinai. Forty thousand Syrians squatted above the Israeli plain on the
Heights of Golan and there was nerve-racking uncertainty over Jordan's true intentions.

Yet no matter how bad things seem, a true calcula-
tion of the situation is usually sacrificed to the public
and political tendency to hope—and therefore believe
—that a solution short of war will be found. We persist
in the belief that war is such a traumatic experience
that men will go to almost any length to avoid it. In
sad fact, there is for every nation a measurable point
at which war, with all of its manifold risks and implications, is preferable to the prevailing situation.

The eighteen-man Israeli Cabinet had been meeting
more or less all day on Sunday, June 4. It had ad-
journed only a few minutes before Mayor Tate's Italian
airliner touched down in the soft, cool evening at Lydda
airport. The late radio news bulletins from Jerusalem
were telling the summer darkness that the Cabinet had
reviewed the security and political situations and had
decided to intensify diplomatic activity in the capitals
of maritime powers; this was activity in accordance with

the first stage of the American plan. There had been a bit of chair-switching to fill out the multi-party government of national unity, according to the Jerusalem radio, and a new Israel bond issue had been approved for presentation to the Knesset the next day.

The appearance created was that of a government which has decided to go on maneuvering and restrain itself for a while. The same impression had been created the day before when General Moshe Dayan, the new defense minister, held a press conference. Diplomacy having begun, he said, and the moment of immediate reaction by military means having passed, diplomacy must be given a chance.

The Israeli government was exercising its undeniable right to deceive in order to disguise its intentions. The deception seemed plausible to the world in general and to the Arabs in particular because no one could understand the particular impact of a series of interrelated events upon the complex Israeli character. Americans, Irishmen and Syrians would undoubtedly have continued to rely on diplomacy at that stage if not forever.

Physically, coastal Israel looks like Florida without the bad taste. The road from Lydda to Tel Aviv is marked by green signs with luminous white letters in Hebrew and Roman characters; they give directions and make the tacit admission that even Israel's best friends can't read her script. On the night of June 4 the wide highways were nearly empty. Automobile headlights picked up rows of thick-foliaged trees and big fields planted with vegetables in neat rows that disappeared into the farther darkness.

Since one is accustomed to thinking of the Holy Land in terms of antiquity, Tel Aviv comes as something of a shock. It is a new city. Consequently, its architecture is derivative of the mid-twentieth century; concert halls and public buildings are in either the cluttered fashion of the 1920's or sheer, post-war angular with lots of brick and glass. Apartment buildings reflect the squared, imitation-Moorish style beloved of the men who designed movie theaters in the 1930's. The city sits on several undulating ridges and sprawls up and down the Mediterranean coast. It is low, flat and subject to constant additions by the restless builders of Israel.

By midnight on Sunday, June 4, the streets were almost empty. A few men leaned against sandbags stacked shoulder high around the corners of apartment buildings. Here and there someone hung over a balcony railing to look into the street. Figures moved behind the taped glass of store fronts.

The deception was working, even on the people of Israel. There were reserve air-force pilots home on leave that evening. No one could have known that the Cabinet had decided, only a few hours before, to go to war. The decision was nearly unanimous. Only two ministers of the left-wing Mapam party had voted no.

The first air-raid siren of the third Arab-Israeli war went off in Tel Aviv at 7:50 a.m. on Monday, June 5. Its sound was a nerve-twisting, nasal howl in the upper register. On the beach below the Tel Aviv Hilton a group of men who had been filling sandbags stopped shoveling, put their hands on their hips and looked off to the south.

It is hard to believe that an air-raid warning means what it implies; when one hears a siren in New York or London, it signifies either an equipment test or a house fire or noon. Exactly what the sirens really meant in Tel Aviv that morning remains a mystery. Were there Egyptian jets on the way to bomb the city, as the Israelis first claimed? Or did the commanders expect retaliation for what they were about to do? Or were the first air-raid warnings a device planned to support the contention that the Egyptians started the war by making an aerial feint toward Israel?

Whatever the explanation, the attackers were sounding warnings as they attacked. A few minutes before the sirens went off, needle-nosed Mirage III's, Mystères and Super-Mystères had lifted with bursts of engine thunder from Israeli airstrips to begin the most extraordinary series of sorties in the history of flying combat. Glinting in the morning sun, they tipped their wings outward in four different directions and roared off to win the war.

Much has been written and there have been many arguments about the aerial tactics designed by Brigadier General Mordecai Hod, the commander of the Israeli air force. At first it was thought that the fighter-bombers that morning ducked under Egyptian radar to make their attacks. Then the theory of a circling sweep out to sea and in behind Egypt's defenses from the west appeared. On a subsequent American television program General Dayan said that there wasn't any sweep out to sea.

The truth seems to lie in a combination of all the theories, just as compromise is the way to truth in many other controversies about the war. Some of the Israeli attackers on the morning of June 5 did streak down the coast and curve inward upon the Egyptian Delta. A few flew west of Egypt and then turned back east. Some of the jets roared straight west across the Sinai, spitting cannon fire and bombs onto the airfields of El Arish, Jebel Libni, Bir Gifgafa and Bir El Thamad. One pilot said later that he flew over the shimmering desert at an altitude of thirty feet. Approaching target, all the Israeli jets flew low and maintained radio silence. The radar equipment supplied to Egypt by the Russians is—con-

trary to popular notion—quite good. But Israeli intelligence had been studying its height capacities and systems of alert for years. The ingoing path of every
fighter-bomber was planned exactly. As well as the four
critically important bases in the Sinai, fourteen other
Egyptian airdromes were hit. Not all the Egyptians
were taken by surprise. Israeli planes were lost to small-
arms fire from the ground and many of the returning
aircraft had bullet holes in their metal skins. The attacks
on Jordanian, Syrian and Iraqi airfields were similarly
designed and executed. The only variations to the technique of low, swift flight, radio silence and precise
marksmanship were those required to accommodate different sorts of terrain. The first air strikes on the morning of June 5 did not win the war by themselves; the
air sorties continued all day and into the next day. The
Iraqi airfield H-3 was not taken out until Tuesday
morning. The sort of flying called for is exhausting to
the nerves, yet some pilots went on seven sorties on the
first day of the war. The ultimate air objective was the
same as the ultimate ground objective—to push back,
to win and to render the Arab war machinery incapable
of combat for a long time to come.

Every war needs a hero or, at least, a heroic group.
The presumed hero of the third Arab-Israeli war was
General Moshe Dayan. While his accomplishments in
both the political and military aspects of the war were
considerable, General Dayan does not fulfill the definition of an ultimate hero—that is, the man without
whom the war would not have ended as it did. That
role belongs to General Mordecai Hod and the planners
of Israel's aerial tactics. General Yitsak Rabin, the chief
of staff, mapped out several choices in over-all strategy.
All of them hung on General Hod's air plan. General
Dayan made the selection of a particular strategy and

re-designed its weakest part—the attack on Jordan. But victory still hung on General Hod's air plan.

The results of this violent explosion of air power would not be known for sixteen hours. The Israelis had good reason for keeping quiet about it. They did not want the United Nations Security Council passing cease-fire resolutions until the Israeli ground attacks had got deep into enemy territory. Nor did they want the Soviet Union entering the war to rescue the Arabs. In this, Cairo Radio co-operated handsomely. Before the sun set on Monday the Egyptians had claimed seventy Israeli aircraft shot down and declared that Tel Aviv was in flames. It was upon this information that the Soviets seemed to base their estimates in the first twelve hours of the war. There were two frightening moments. The Israeli embassy in Paris leaked news of the real situation on the morning of the first day; and, for some inexplicable reason, the Israeli radio claimed, in an Arabic-language broadcast, that 120 Egyptian, Syrian and Jordanian aircraft had been destroyed. In his second announcement of the day the Israeli army spokesman made an exquisite gyration which deflected but did not exactly deny the blurted truth. The Paris and Kol Israel announcements, he roared, were "premature, unclear and utterly unauthorized."

In Tel Aviv the only evidence of war was the morbid howl of air-raid sirens.

And—for the first half-hour—hardly anyone quite believed it. The workmen on the beach had gone back to their shoveling. The sun was bright and the sky was without clouds, haze or approaching aircraft. Cars moved at normal speed along the main road that paralleled the shore line. By some acquired inner sense of the dramatic, we expect the arrival of great and fatal events to be accompanied by suitable exterior signs—

darkening sky, falling barometer and cries of alarm. When such signs are absent and we are told that a war has begun, the tranquil landscape about us has a macabre look of unreality as if it and not the war were out of place. A correspondent who had arrived from Rome the night before telephoned a colleague one floor up in the Tel Aviv Hilton to ask what the air-raid sirens meant.

"I don't know," the other reporter said. "This has never happened before."

"Do you suppose it could really be the war?"

"How the hell should I know?"

The Hilton had been nearly emptied by the exodus of tourists as the crisis hotted up. The management, with typically sanguine Israeli logic, had decided to keep its journalist guests on the first six stories because the Egyptians were bad pilots and might bump into the upper floors of the hotel by accident.

The cry of sirens abruptly stopped and the hushed moment between warning and all-clear hovered over the brilliant morning. In that new silence, war finally seemed possible. When the sirens go quiet, reconstruction of the immediate past is applied to speculation about the moment, and the tendency is to get one's trousers on fast and make it to the ground floor of the hotel as quickly as possible. Fear had begun.

At 8:30 Michael Hadow, Britain's elegant and cryptic ambassador to Israel, appeared in the Hilton lobby. Reporters asked him if he knew what was going on. "I don't know a thing except that I'm going to have breakfast," Hadow answered. He smiled. "It's probably only a skirmish."

For those correspondents who couldn't speak Hebrew and who therefore were unable to understand the announcements of the Israeli radio, the first hard confirmation that war had actually begun came from taxi drivers who took newsmen to the press center three miles away from the Hilton as soon as the all-clear sounded. "Thank God!" one of them said. "Now we shall have a war and now it will be all right!"

The taxi radio was speaking in short bursts of mellifluous phrases. These were the poetic Hebrew code words that summoned reservists to pre-planned mobilization points. The call-ups had been rehearsed so many times that the poetry of the code was lost in a jangle of exasperation. Now, suddenly, the phrases had a brittle clarity. The streets of central Tel Aviv were filling up with traffic. In the bright morning, reservists were rushing to their units in or on anything that had wheels. "Zion," said the radio, "Open Letter." A man flew by on a motor scooter, stuffing his shirt into his trousers while he steered and held a rifle and a helmet with his other hand. "Wedding March," Kol Israel intoned, "Love."

The press center was a two-story building with an inner court garden of trees and grass, writing rooms for reporters and a big hall where most of the war's briefings and press conferences were held. There was also a bar, which served abominable dry sandwiches that no one minded. On the second floor there were two offices where briefing officers worked, slept and received journalists between scheduled press conferences.

The first official announcement of the war was posted on bulletin boards before 9:00 a.m. It was brief and chilling in its understatement of the way Israel's third moment of mortal history had begun.

> The Israel Army spokesman announces today:
> Since the early hours of this morning heavy fighting has been taking place on the southern front

between Egyptian armored and aerial forces which moved against Israel, and our forces went into action in order to check them.

There was no elaboration. Armies, which engage in mankind's supreme physical adventure, write mankind's dullest prose.

A little later a military briefing was held in the up-stairs hall. While traffic streamed by on the street below and men trotted on the sidewalks to their destinations of mobilization, an officer propped up a map and ex-plained that the Israeli early-warning system had, that morning, spotted a two-pronged air attack. Egyptian jets had been seen approaching the seacoast from the west, which might mean an attack on air bases and population centers. In conjunction with this there were armored movements toward the Negev-Sinai border. A correspondent asked where the ground attack had started. The location, said the officer, was secret. At the moment, he said, an armored battle was raging in the south. "We plan to be reticent about details. We can't say too much for security reasons. Let Nasser do the guessing."

The cutting howl of an air-raid siren lifted from si-lence into ear-shattering sound. The traffic in the street immediately stopped. Cars pulled over to the curbs and the sidewalks were suddenly empty.

As the siren—located close by—yowled, the briefing officer leaned on his pointer and looked out the window. He was a middle-aged blond major. He had blue eyes and a patient smile. The siren stopped. "Foreign minis-try and military briefings will take place in this room twice a day," the officer said. "We are trying to arrange trips to the battle front and you will have to sign up for these. Please write down your name and the name of your organization."

"Can we go today?" someone shouted.

The major smiled his good-man smile. "We'll see. Be patient with us."

He launched into a discussion of the history that had preceded the war, of the quality of roads in the Sinai Desert, the strategic importance of El Arish on the coast and the various distances involved in pushing armies to the Suez Canal and beyond. The location of Mount Sinai, he added helpfully, is not exactly known.

At ten o'clock Prime Minister Levi Eshkol went on the radio to address the Israeli nation. "There may be cruel and bloody days of struggle," he said. "In these days all the people are the army and all the country is the front." For a moment the profound differences between two Jewish characters had been bridged by the violence of war's arrived truth. "In this hour," said Premier Eshkol, "we note the growing declarations of identification with Israel expressed by our people of the Diaspora. The Jewish people siding with Israel give us comfort and hope." The difference was stated and, in the stating, ceased to exist.

Soldiers are afraid because they are the specific objects of the enemy's extermination plan. They draw their reassurance from the fact of their numbers and from the fact that they are moving. People in the cities of a country at war are afraid because they are trapped in a motionless target; the violence disgorged upon them is general. Its authors hope to kill everyone and destroy everything. No man really believes that he will be a primary target; the fear of people in the cities is that they will perish by accidentally standing in the way of someone else's intended fate.

When a city is waiting to be bombed, its inhabitants think frantically of its geography; what parts are likely to be hit first? Photographs of cities that have been bombed flash across the mind—Cologne, one mass of rubble; London with this or that street blasted and others untouched; the burning railroad yards of Shanghai. The conclusion is reached that bombing is an imprecise art at best and that bombs are likely to fall anywhere in the city. The waiters look at the structures around them and try to estimate how they would collapse. Outward into the street? Inward upon themselves? The photographs of bombed cities show both sorts of destruction. In their minds the waiting people dash back and forth, looking for the safest place. The beach? Machine-gun bullets. The center of the boulevard? Shell fragments or a direct hit. Bomb shelters? The fear of being entombed alive is especially vivid.

Shame and envy become involved in the process of waiting. The all-clear sounds and a girl comes out of a building. She walks away, looking casually into shopwindows and lifting her face into the sun. Surely she is as much aware of the danger as the one who watches her. Yet she is so casual! The observer envies her simplicity of being—perhaps it is just a low-key chemistry—and, at the same time, he is ashamed of himself for all the symptoms of his fear. An ice battery has charged his nerves until the smallest sudden sound makes him jerk with apprehension and perspiration soaks his back and armpits. The palms of his hands are wet. However much he fancies himself a creature of philosophic thoughts, his mind, during the waiting, does not concern itself with the meaning of death but only with its procedures.

All around him people appear to be concentrating on what is being said. He tries to focus his own mind on the words and to forget that the city has lost any identity except that of an instrument of its own and his own destruction.

"We have attacked air bases," the major said, "and we are, of course, giving air support to the ground forces." He explained that the Gaza Strip was a primary target in the ground war. "It is a gun pointed at Tel Aviv and the trigger of the gun is Rafah junction at the west end of the strip. There are two or three hundred thousand Palestinian refugees bottled up in there. They are vicious, dangerous and they have nothing to lose." He said that nearly full mobilization was on in Israel.

Outside on the street a truck rumbled past. It was smeared with dun-colored mud and carried a sign: COFFEE IN CAIRO AT NOON. ICE CREAM IN DAMASCUS IN THE EVENING.

The major announced that Abba Eban would hold a press conference at the center around one o'clock. The correspondents went downstairs to the courtyard or back into the writing rooms to begin their dispatches. In moments of tension and uncertainty a journalist goes to his typewriter; there was very little to write at that hour, but it seemed incongruous to be in the middle of an earth-jarring event and not to write.

Some of the reporters went out onto the steps of the building to watch the vehicles rushing men off to their units. Israeli journalists hugged transistor radios to their ears, switching from Kol Israel to the Arab radio stations. Arabic is the second language of Israel, and a good many of the local press speak it fluently. Reporters from Europe and North America shouted for translation every time the Israelis laughed or murmured in surprise at something said on the radio. At 11:40 Cairo announced that Israel had been attacked and—five minutes later—that the Syrians were moving in from the north. Like the Israeli claim that Egyptian ground and air movements toward Israel had started the war, this claim of a Syrian invasion was not often heard again after the first morning of fighting.

A reservist lieutenant colonel from the briefing office upstairs came out on the steps and said that the Jordanians had opened fire on Jerusalem at 11:45. It appeared that a second front had begun.

It is ironic that Jordan should have played the key role in starting the war and that she should have caused the Israelis such tension and uncertainty during it. Jordan, along with Lebanon, is a moderate Israeli neighbor. Before the war the government in Jerusalem held King Hussein in a sort of affectionate contempt. The Israeli hope never quite died that some sort of realistic neighborhood arrangement might be made with the young Hashemite monarch. After the war was over, Hussein had become the most hated Arab leader from the Israeli point of view. "The stupid bastard knew better," said one Israeli general with a vernacular grasp of American idiom. The hatred for Hussein was that special sort reserved for a fool who has been gulled into doing evil.

Hussein's own feelings mirrored those of the Israelis; the King of Jordan had continued to nourish secret hopes of a modus vivendi with Israel. He had inherited the notion from his grandfather, Abdullah. In the war, Jordan's losses were the heaviest in practical terms— she suffered the highest percentage of troops killed and equipment destroyed. The loss of the West Bank to Israel meant that the greater part of Jordan's arable land was gone, and, in being driven from Jerusalem, King Hussein lost the tourist revenues which were his largest source of foreign income aside from foreign aid.

Early in the morning of June 5 the Israelis had sent two messages to Hussein. The first, from Abba Eban, urged the King to stay out of the battle. The second—

from Premier Eshkol and delivered personally in Amman by General Odd Bull of the United Nations—repeated the plea: if Jordan would stay out of the war as she had done in 1956, she wouldn't be hurt. When the Jordanian artillery opened up on Jerusalem and on the Israeli villages of Sandala and Nehusha after eleven o'clock on the morning of June 5, the Israelis were convinced that Hussein was only giving token support to the Egyptians and the Syrians. Even when the Arab Legion entered the demilitarized zone between the two sectors of Jerusalem and drove the United Nations Truce Supervisory people out of the old residence of the British High Commissioner, the Israelis limited themselves to re-taking the position. They did not attack the Old City of Jerusalem that day. Nor did they move forward anywhere along the Jordanian front during the first day. Israeli artillery engaged in thundering duels with the Jordanians, but the only offensive action came from the air when Israeli Mirage III's and Mystères knocked out Jordanian fields. It wasn't until long after darkness had fallen on the first twelve hours of the war that Israel finally reached the conclusion that Jordan was in the fight to the finish and so moved forward to finish her. This restraint is another of the war's mysteries. General Rabin's strategy apparently included only contingency plans for a battle with Jordan. General Dayan's principal strategic contribution was the brilliant campaign against King Hussein's Arab Legion. Perhaps on that first day the Israelis didn't move because the plan wasn't ready. Or perhaps it simply required a day of fighting to persuade them that Hussein was serious.

Political decisions are required as a war is being fought. The making of such decisions was another important contribution by General Dayan. Though a loner in politics, he knew the way the Cabinet worked—he had served in it as minister of agriculture—and though he has a certain contempt for the labyrinthine processes of politics, Moshe Dayan is perfectly aware of the relationship between choice and implication. Until he became defense minister in the week before the war, that portfolio was held by Premier Eshkol. The practical effect was to put the bulk of the decision-making upon General Rabin, who was chief of staff. General Rabin knew that he was incapable of political judgment, and General Dayan's arrival in the forefront of events came to him as a relief. The two generals are not friends.

The most important political decisions were the one that stopped the advancing Israeli armies on the east bank of the Suez Canal and the one that swept the Jordanian West Bank into the Israeli geographic net. The taking of the Gaza Strip was a military necessity and the seizure of Jerusalem was an emotional inevitability. Had King Hussein limited himself to token support for Egypt and Syria, one political decision would not have been necessary and one emotional inevitability would not have presented itself.

Hussein claimed later that this was not the case. When Israel blasted his airfields, he said, he had no choice but to fight. Yet it was the degree of Jordan's response that was her undoing.

On that first morning the role of Jordan was uncertain and the bewildering crash power of the Israelis was hurtling itself into the massed Egyptian forces in the Sinai Desert. Such was the magnitude of this second Israeli Sinai campaign in eleven years that certain clichés of image sprang up to explain its outcome; the ferocious, victory-crying Jew was one of them, and the cowardly Egyptian fleeing in panic was another. The second cliché is closer to the truth than the first. There *were* Egyptians who fought well—especially officers;

unfortunately for President Nasser and for the Arab problem in squaring verbal reality with the other sort, there weren't enough of them.

As to the first cliché, the Israelis in combat are not soldiers of rage or arrogance. They plan with an inexhaustible passion for detail and fight with brilliant drive. But the fighting is done in a curious attitude of muscular doubt, as if the Israelis could not take confidence from the unfolding evidence of their own achievements. In his book *Fin du Peuple Juif,* Georges Friedmann speaks of the gift of anxiety which is part of the intrinsic Jewish legacy. While the Israelis are struggling back toward the pre-Diasporic Jewish identity, this element of anxiety remains to some degree or other. In order to understand the extraordinary fighting capacities of the Israeli armies it becomes necessary to understand what the Israeli is anxious about. Naturally, he fears death. But there is a deeper, subliminal anxiety which, since it exists below the level of personal awareness, exerts a primordial and terrible pressure upon these who fight. For the Israelis victory means only a continuation of the status quo—perhaps, at best, a continuation in a slightly better form. Defeat, on the other hand, would literally mean an end of Jewish being. The armies of Israel are hounded by an inner vision of Armageddon. The armies of the Arabs are intoxicated with a giddy notion of what victory would mean. He who expects to be annihilated in every sense of the word fights more zealously than he who hopes to restore his pride by winning.

The Israeli vision of Armageddon is not concious, nor is it apocalyptic in the accepted sense of the word. If it is true, as Carl Jung maintains, that we are born with memories of the existence that preceded us, then we are aware of certain implications. For nineteen cen-

turies the Jews lived in the world as strangers. Implicit
in their alienated life was the idea of returning to the
status of acceptability. For centuries this concept of a
return was vague. It was deflected briefly at the end of
the eighteenth century when the French revolution decreed the emancipation of the Jews. Acceptability
seemed, briefly, to lie in assimilation. Clermont-Ton-
nerre had said, "To the Jews as human beings—everything. To the Jews as a nation—nothing." When emancipation failed, the concept of a return to acceptability
assumed the specific form of Zionism, Theodor Herzl's
vision of a Jewish National Homeland. The ancient
prayers hinging upon a restoration of the Land of
Canaan suddenly had a concrete reality. Twice the Jews
had been expelled from Palestine. During the second
exile they had been persecuted by pogroms, denied
citizenship almost everywhere and victimized by Hitler's
monstrous and humiliating Endlösung—the final solution to the Jewish question. In the twentieth century the
struggle turned itself upon Palestine; the Zionist drive
to return became unrelenting and obsessive and the
Promised Land was regained. The eternal Jewish question, "Why us?" had been answered. The state of Israel
justifies nineteen centuries of prayer and suffering; it
makes everything else that happened assume a logic.
Israel became the direction in which the Jews had been
moving for the two millennia, and without it Jewish
Diasporic history would have no meaning—to the Israelis.

Thus, it follows that if the Israelis lose Israel, if they
are driven from it a third time, then history becomes
meaningless again. A third return is unthinkable, especially in a world whose Western civilizations have
been purged of the worst impulses of anti-Semitism.
Deep in the Israeli conciousness all of this is recognized.

To lose again means to go into the world forever, to assimilate and cease to be.

This is the inner vision of Armageddon that hounds the Israeli soldier, filling him full of the tensions that explode with such force; it is a collective tension and its energies burst in simultaneous wrath upon the enemy. It is for this that the sun stands still as the Israelis go to war.

Racked with anxiety, fueled with tension, the armies of Israel flung themselves into the desert on the morning of June 5. They took extraordinary chances. Bursting into the Gaza Strip toward Khan Yunis on the coast, the armored brigades rolled over minefields that they knew were there. Though two other armored units smashed into the Sinai, this northernmost force under the command of Brigadier General Israel Tal covered the most territory and reached, that first day, the first key Egyptian stronghold—El Arish. General Tal's units, drawn from the Seventh Israeli Armored Brigade, divided themselves several different times and actually fought in three different directions—west to Khan Yunis, north toward the ancient Philistine city of Gaza where Samson pulled down the temple, while the remainder of General Tal's tanks broke out of the Gaza Strip through Rafah and into the Sinai as far as El Arish, the coastal enclave whose name, in Arabic, means "The Fruitful."

This west-driving armored unit made a mistake that was a projection of Israeli military virtue. The whole desert fighting plan was based on speed and a momentum that continued without stopping until the western limit of the fighting was achieved—the Suez Canal. In its savage momentum, General Tal's armored unit simply by-passed El Arish, going to either side as the juggernaut rolled out along the coastal road. Large

numbers of Egyptians were, in effect, bottled up in the
coastal town. They had time to recover from the stun-
ning impact of the original assault, and when the Israelis
returned to take El Arish the fighting was severe and
the losses were considerable.

Coming out of the Gaza Strip, the Israelis encoun-
tered an Egyptian tank company at a crossroads two
kilometers west of Rafah. A ferocious fire-fight ensued
in which two thirds of the Arab vehicles were destroyed.
Mirage III's and Super-Mystères screeched overhead
like enraged mother hawks. Farther down the road to
El Arish, Egyptian troops in cinder-block trenches, in
tanks, trucks, half-tracks and tented bivouacs, heard the
hysterical radio chatter of their colleagues engaging the
Israelis at the crossroads. As the fighter bombers came
hurtling across the landscape, spraying cannon, machine-gun and rocket fire in the searing sunlight, the
Egyptians had the sudden vision of an onslaught so
powerful and inevitable that nothing could stop it.
They leaped out of the trenches and down from the
vehicles and began to run—toward the coast or over the
dunes that banked the road on the south side. Machine-
gun bullets ripped their brown flesh apart, snapping
backbones and splintering ribs and limbs; stalled trucks
hit by cannon fire exploded, flinging their fleeing drivers
head over heels into the sand. One man, soaked with
burning petrol, ran screaming for fifty feet before he
triggered a mine which blew him into two pieces. On
the outskirts of El Arish, rocket fire tore into a muni-
tions train parked on a railroad siding. It blew up with
such violence that an Egyptian officer standing in his
tank turret one hundred yards away was broken in two.
The dark angel of every human dream had spread its
shadow upon the Sinai and there was no place to hide.

In the central part of the northern desert, Brigadier

General Ariel Sharon's tanks had burst into the Sinai to halt and then reverse the Egyptian units poised to go up the Nitzana road toward Beersheba. On the southern Sinai front the armored forces of Brigadier General Avraham Yoffe had begun a looping thrust into the wilderness toward El Thamad; after two days of ferocious battles General Yoffe's force would join up with General Sharon's and the combined unit would herd the remnant Egyptians west into a flaming trap at the Mitla Pass.

At 4:00 a.m. Washington time, Secretary of State Rusk was called to the State Department and told what had happened. He dispatched a telegram to Soviet foreign minister Andrei Gromyko saying that the United States was staying strictly out of the fighting. By noon a similar message had come from Moscow to the White House. In those few hours each of the potential detonators of the third world war had been assured that the other would not move first.

Before dawn a group of senior diplomats had assembled in the Department's operations room to read the incoming and still unverified progress reports. If the war they had struggled for so long to avert had exploded out of their control, it was at least going the right way. Diplomatic sophistication gave way to jubilation. To one group, Eugene Rostow, the Undersecretary of State for Political Affairs, said, "Come on, fellows, remember we're neutral in thought, word and deed." This quote from Woodrow Wilson was received with laughter by the men in the room—but it took some explaining when it became public.

At the press center in Tel Aviv the correspondents felt tense and stupid as they sat on the grass and listened to the radio. A third air-raid alert went off at 12:35.

The Middle East was, quite obviously, the center of the world and Tel Aviv was the center of the center. Yet it was impossible to confirm anything. Having filed the first bulletins that a war had started, the correspondents could now envision their editors dancing in frustrated rage at the lack of details. Rumors were swimming in the hot air—the Israelis had appealed to the Egyptian commander at El Arish to give up because he had nothing left (did that mean that all the airfields were wiped out?), Haifa had been bombed, the number of Arab aircraft destroyed was 100 . . . 175 . . . 300. . . . The briefing officers clearly knew something and it was clearly something good. They were hardly able to suppress their delight, but if asked specific questions, they answered, "When the proper time comes, when Colonel Pearlman holds his briefing here tonight, it will be even more fantastic than you or I could imagine."

Cairo Radio said that Tel Aviv was in flames.

At 1:50 Abba Eban appeared at the press center and the correspondents rushed up to the briefing hall.

The foreign minister of Israel has the look and manner of a chubby, middle-aged boy. His slicked-back hair and earnest, corpulent facial expressions give Abba Eban the eternal appearance of a third-former protesting to the senior prefect about the injustices of extra study hall or the inferior quality of breakfast buns. He is not only an extremely articulate man, but he can unroll his unique gift for phraseology in Hebrew, English, Arabic, French and German. He repeated to the correspondents that it was Egypt's aerial and ground stabs at Israel earlier that morning which had caused the war that was now raging full-blown in the desert. Then, as if this were an irrelevance which he hardly expected anyone to believe, Eban said, "Never in history has there been such a righteous use of armed force."

Another air-raid siren shattered the attention of the reporters in the briefing hall. Abba Eban did not seem to notice. He is a devotee of the Israeli cult of unflinchableness.

"Israel," he said, "is entitled to the support and charity of all peace-loving nations."

Nobody knows who the Jews are. Nobody has ever really known, and the Jews themselves are just now trying to decide. Their origins are lost in the history that took place before literature, the history that was already ancient when the Nile people reproduced themselves in stone, paint and wood in order to be remembered. Before that, human chronology is smothered in darkness and silence, and somewhere in it the Jews began.

From that enigma of time the tribes of Hebrew people approach us first in the twentieth century before Christ, moving out of Ur of the Chaldees into northwestern Mesopotamia. The world in which they appear is savage and hungry and bound in a peculiar rigidity by laws, cults and gods whose origins are as mysterious as those of the people they command. Two centuries later, harassed by hunger, enemies and the other forces that motivate the migrations of tribal peoples, the Hebrews moved west. Some stopped and separated into factions of petty rivalry on the fertile coast of the eastern Mediterranean while others, went farther, into the rich Egyptian Delta. There, as the dynasties rose and fell in varying climates of authority and faith, the fortunes of the Hebrews deteriorated until by the time Moses led them back to the eastern coast in the middle of the thirteenth century B.C. they had been reduced to embittered battalions of forced laborers.

In every people the power to be great is resident, but not every people fulfills this potentiality for glory; some die, some stop before the summit is attained, some turn upon themselves and crush the ephemeral capacity in rages of self-destruction.

But if greatness is ever achieved, it is never forgotten. The memory of it persists and the subsequent history of the people who once achieved themselves is dictated by how they use the memory of their greatness. In the centuries between the return to the northern fertile crescent and the death of King David, the Hebrews became Jews and fulfilled their capacity to be great.

The land into which they had thrust themselves was the ancient province of the Canaanites. It took the Jews three hundred years to destroy and absorb them. In the eleventh century a new people appeared from the sea—probably from Crete—and built the great coastal cities of Gaza and Ashkelon. The Jews and the Philistines threw themselves upon each other with a ferocity that was triggered by an instinctive knowledge that the land could not support both intruders.

As they warred and evolved toward their moment of ultimate greatness, the Jews grew in sophistication. They began to come together through their common struggles, they began to feel an ethnically cohesive people's demand for a warrior king. The first one was Saul of the tribe of Benjamin, erratic, half mad and so incapable in some ways that he nearly arrested the process which the Jews were undergoing. History, however, seems to pay special attention to a people at such delicate moments and it managed to save the Jews from being damaged by Saul.

He was succeeded by his son-in-law, armor-bearer

and hated rival, David—one of the most complex men
of history. Deeply religious, adulterous, magnetic, capable of treachery, poetic, wise and gifted with a
prophetic vision of the approaching moment, David
became king of Judah, based upon Hebron; he united
the tribes that remained autonomous, captured Jerusalem and made it the capital of the nation he had created, as well as the City of God. King David is worthy
of the almost endless analyses that have been written
about him. Like the Prophet Mohammed, he was not
a saint. Perhaps saints are not the proper people to
create nations. King David created the Jews. He delivered them to the doorway of their greatness.

From the moment marked by King David's voyage
across history, the Jews began to recede from their
maximum temporal greatness—that physical summation
of military supremacy, unchallenged security in the
world and internal harmony that is usually taken to be
the height of national accomplishment. Fractionaliza-
tion, a bitter knowledge of the power that lay beyond
the ken of their Canaanite world and the dark ignominy
of dwindling strength awaited the Jews in the eight and
a half centuries that unraveled from the death of King
David to the birth of Christ. The single kingdom broke
into two: Israel and Judah. The former was destroyed
by the Assyrians in 721 B.C. and the latter disintegrated
under the onslaughts of foreign power, the coming of
the Greeks, revolts, quarrels, the rise of imperial Rome
in the East and the final expulsion that was the Diaspora.

But the memory remained. And if it is true that the
Jews are the chosen of God, a particular gift was the
Chooser's tangible legacy. A genius of the spirit rose
in the Jewish character as the power to be one nation
declined. Jerusalem became less important as the seat

of temporal strength than as the city of the great temples of God—the first built by Solomon, son of David, and the second begun by a man named Sheshbazzar about whom nothing else is known. God—if, indeed, He was guiding Jewish fortunes during the decline— even provided a laboratory of time in which the Jews could blend the spiritual strength that was to keep them intact as a people during the desperate and tragic centuries of exile. In the fifth century Judea was conquered by the Babylonians, and the Jews went into a brief, preliminary diaspora. It was during this so-called Babylonic exile that the amassed texts of Jewish history and revelation began to develop into a code of law that governed secular life as well as religious practice. The authors of the Old Testament Chronicles also shaped the books of Ezra and Nehemiah as we know them now. Ezra as the Sopher—literally, Author of the Law of the God of Heaven—was one of the vessels of the completed code as well as the leader of the Jews of Babylon back to Judea. When the first exile was over, Judaism was no longer defensible by the sword but, in the minds of the Jews, by the Torah, the Pentateuch or law of Moses, which is the first five books of the Bible.

The beginnings of modern history churned through the Land of Canaan and the Romans could no longer be bothered with putting down the revolts that kept breaking out in their Palestinian colony. By the middle of the second century of the Christian era the Jews were scattered—they were resident, according to the reckonings of historians, in every town in the Roman empire.

But beneath the sustaining genius for spirit, and beneath the law that kept the spirit intact, there remained deep in the Jewish unconscious the memory of the time of David, as the Arabs remembered Aiyamu-Arab. The difference was that the Jews progressed forward

in time along another route while the spirituality of the
Arabs remained anchored in nostalgia for one moment
in the past. For the Jews, the process of self-rediscovery
was postponed for nineteen hundred years; a new Jewish personality was shaped by alienation, by the bigotry
and fear of the people among whom the Jews lived in
exile. But the exiles remembered what they had been.
In Babylon they had sat by the rivers and wept when
they remembered Zion. But during the Diaspora of
nearly two millennia the cry of the exiles became militant. "If I forget thee, O Jerusalem," raged the Jews in
their darkness and despair, "let my right hand forget
her cunning." It is the right hand that steers the plow
and kills.

Who shall properly consider the Diaspora and describe it with balance? What Christian can dispassion-
ately tell of the witless hatred, barbaric fear, super-
stition, the bloody fantasies and sports of murder, expulsion, torture and harassment with which his people
treated the Jews? What Jew can calmly say that it no
longer matters that *his* people lived in a ceaseless history of injury as exquisite as the taunting caricature of
Shakespeare's Shylock and as gross as the chain-whop-
ping death of Russia's pious, slobbering Black Hundreds? Who shall say with relieved equanimity that
now the world knows better, when—despite centuries
of Jewish cries of anguish and the implorings of decent
Christians—the final lesson that anti-Semitism is an
offense in the very eye of God had to be taught through
the final solution of the arch-maniac Adolf Hitler?
Western civilization has nothing with which to redeem
itself of the offense it perpetrated upon the Jews—not
the Emancipation of 1791, because it failed; not the
remembered revulsion of men like Emile Zola, because
the nasty hatred of a hundred Voltaires balances it and

more; not Wilhelm Dohm's courageous and scholarly
Concerning the Civic Amelioration of the Jews, because
its decent appeal is smothered in the forged rubbish of
The Protocols of the Elders of Zion; even the pious
Papal hand-washing of non possumus endured until
the extravagance of Hitler made it uncomfortable to
keep looking the other way. In Britain and the United
States the Jews—in Goethe's phrase—had it better.
But even the best of democracies cannot legislate
against the legends, fantasies and knee-jerk prejudice
bred by the bestial history of the Diaspora.

The effect of centuries of such treatment was understandable. Into the Jewish nature there was instilled
that sense of anxiety which is deeper and more enduring
than any personal insecurity could ever be. The Jew
considered himself helpless in the world—and all the
evidence supported his assumption. Upon the anxiety
there was laid the particular sense of shame that comes
with the frustrated knowledge that one cannot defend
oneself and one's kind. At times the shame welled over
into rebellion—Yad Mordecai's Warsaw ghetto uprising is a classic of the decision to die for a lion instead
of a lamb. But, for the most part, the Jew bowed his
head before his Christian tormentors, took it and be-
wailed his fate. Shame is the progenitor of anger, and
the inherited, stifled anger of the Jews grew through
the generations, nurtured, perhaps, by the dim memory
of the warrior kings and the earthbound victors of Zion.
If he could not find compensation in the physical history
of his Diaspora, the Jew could justify his existence
through the works of his mind and the creations of his
artistry.

And so a new Jewish character was created. It was
bred of bits of Germany, Eastern Europe and Russia,
and of the multiplying laws of the Talmud which had

the effect of isolating the Jew even further from his hostile neighbors; the ghetto became as much a matter of convenience for the practice of the strict rules of Judaism as a cultural fortress against the gentile world. The Jew of the Diaspora emerged—Yiddish-speaking, bent with his sufferings, endlessly seeking a negotiated way out since he had nothing to fight with, going resignedly to his doom when his wit failed, the intellectual, the hoarder of tangible wealth since land was often denied him. Christian civilization, having tortured and pounded the character of the Jew into a form so alien that it glared with its difference, proceeded to shriek with laughter and spit with scorn upon the being that had been so molded. Shylock cavorted for the amusement of illiterate Elizabethans, and Fagin the Thief was offered to the Victorians as a mixed bag of Jewish caricature. The Jew, hearing the laughter and wet with spit, must have hated the prototype himself.

It was the worst thing that had ever happened to a people; it lasted longer, bit deeper and changed more than any other persecution of any other so-called minority. But—if survival is a virtue—it was the best thing that happened to the Jews, too. By their expulsion from the Land of Canaan they continued to be. The Canaanites, the Philistines and the rest of the people in that earlier history were relegated to the archaeological rubbish heaps of history. Because he had been exiled to Europe, the Jew learned the technology and arts of his tormentors. The cruel challenge thrown at him, the dare to survive, charged his stubbornness and electrified his faith, and they made survival possible.

But it was survival in shame and fermenting anger; the Jewish genius for tenacity latched itself onto the political struggle of Zionism, and at last the Jew went home to Palestine and turned it into Israel.

He was racked with memory. Once upon that withered land he had fulfilled the prescription of destiny, he had been a dominating master of the earth. When the Jewish refugees from Eastern Europe trudged back to Palestine in the first quarter of the twentieth century, the memory flickered a little brighter. A comparison of the Jew that had once been with the tortured shape of the Jew that had been created in exile produced a reaction that was, in effect, the beginning of a new and yet very old secular faith. Redemption from the thing that centuries of humiliation had done to them seemed to lie in the working of land and in physical exertion expended in a useful way. The stooped intellectuals of the European ghettos straightened themselves and plunged into the task of making the desert bloom, of draining swamps and pounding rocks from the blistering hills into gravel for roadbeds and house foundations.

This was the first stirring of the attractive puritanism of Israel—the shared life of physical toil and cultural enrichment that developed into the kibbutz movement with its elementary socialism, its Rousseau-like return to the land and the cheerful, hardy character of its proponent, the kibbutznik.

The new life incorporated everything that was opposite to the unhappy existence of the Diaspora. The Jews exchanged the cultured cities of Europe for the raw landscape of the Middle East; they closed down their shops, put aside the pen of the clerk or the journalist and became farmer-soldiers—they restored their manhood and they re-discovered the ability to fight back; the resigned character of the Jewish intellectual who went, head bowed, to his fate evolved in one generation into the rugged nature of the tough Israeli sabra—the one actually born in Israel, whose name, in Hebrew, means "the heart of the cactus."

The inherited anger of many generations burst forth in a fierce determination that never, never again would the Jews be hounded or persecuted, never again would strangers dictate the conditions under which Jews would live. Though not an arrogant people by nature, the Israelis developed a streak of military self-identification; while they do not seek wars, the fighting of them seems to be a form of reassurance as well as a profound source of grief. It is a contradiction that reflects both Jewish characters.

In a way that they barely realized themselves, the Jews of Israel had begun to re-discover themselves in history. They were groping back toward the remembered moment of Davidic greatness, toward the nation of warriors that had commanded the world from the Judean hills and the fastness of Jerusalem. Once, when talking to Adlai Stevenson, David Ben-Gurion gestured toward the Old City of Jerusalem, then still in Jordanian hands, and said, "What is Zionism without Zion?" Jerusalem was a symbol of the time before the Torah became the law that preserved the people; it was a symbol of a time when the Jews had preserved themselves with the temporal power of David and Solomon.

In Israel tensions developed between the Hassidim— the Jews who believe that strict practice and faith are the only sources of Jewish identity—and the tough pioneers who had defined themselves through land, war and sweat. Tensions also developed between the kibbutznikim and those who lead what is called "the other life"—the life of the cities, with all of its evocation of the hateful, Diasporic past.

At times one thinks of Israel as a big summer camp where the emphasis is on sport-shirt informality, a passion for culture and an outdoor life organized into useful work. This is not all of Israel, but it is the part

which attracts outsiders; in the kibbutz movement there
is that return to the elemental for which we all yearn—
the existence we had as children before we knew what
our tensions were or how isolated our lives had become
from the reasons for living them.

Having returned home, the Jews of Israel wandered
deep into the ancient Land of Canaan, back toward its
Davidic history, back to the point in time when, by
Jewish definition, the Jews were great. Those who remained in the Diaspora outside of Israel were proceeding in another direction that Western civilization in its
remorse and shame had opened to them—the direction
of acceptability in the world.

By the evening of June 5 the briefing officers at the
press headquarters in Tel Aviv could hardly contain
themselves. From what they let drop in an excess of
glee, from driblets of radio report and from rumors that
circulated after Israeli editors had been filled in for
their morning editions, it had become apparent that the
Israelis had done unbelievable and marvelous things in
the first ten hours of fighting. It also appeared that es-
calation had been quick but limited. Israeli troops had
crossed into the demilitarized zone to re-take Government House, the headquarters of the United Nations
Truce Supervisory team. Artillery had opened up all
along the Jordanian front. Still the Israelis did not
move. There was heavy shelling from the Syrian heights,
and Syrian aircraft had bombed the area of Haifa Bay
and elsewhere along the upper Israeli coast. Just as
Israel restrained herself on their borders, neither Syria
nor Jordan had made any move to penetrate Israel with
troop movements. It was obvious even from the scattered information on Monday evening that the war
would be won in the air and upon the cruel terrain of

the Sinai. News of the Sinai progress was blacked out; there weren't even any rumors about how it was going in the desert.

By sundown apprehension had slacked off at the press center and in Tel Aviv generally. There had been seven air alerts and yet no bombers had appeared. By that time nearly everyone assumed that none of the immediate Arab belligerents was in any condition to bomb the city. Worry lingered over the Algerian air force— said to be the third largest in Africa after Egypt and the Republic of South Africa.

Word was put out that Colonel Moshe Pearlman, the spokesman of the defense ministry, would brief in mid-evening. Several correspondents decided to go back to the Hilton for dinner. Tel Aviv was under total blackout. Even traffic signals had been switched off. The only automobile headlights permitted were ones painted over in opaque blue—and even they were allowed only quick flicks.

The small group of reporters had gotten half a block away from the press headquarters when the sound of distant cannon began to thump in the star-sprayed darkness. The eighth air-raid warning of the day went off in a rising, piercing yowl. The correspondents dashed back to the press building and went down into its basement shelter for the first time that day. Army girls from the briefing offices, civilians and reporters were sitting in the whitewashed cellar under a network of ceiling pipes. Overhead the boom of cannon grew louder. The lights went off. Someone said, in German, "Air raid," and another voice in English said, "The Jordanian bastards! They're shelling us!" The army girls began to sing a brisk and cheerful song in delicate rondels of contrapuntal Hebrew.

The lights went back on.

The army girls laughed. Their singing had seemed more a way to pass time than to bolster spirits. A blonde, middle-aged woman sitting in a chair asked one of the reporters for a cigarette. Her accent was American. The reporter asked her how long she had been in Israel. She smiled. "I came here from Pittsburgh a hundred years ago. How do you like our war?" A discussion about aerial tactics began and someone said that perhaps Tel Aviv hadn't been bombed because the Israelis had threatened to destroy Egypt's High Aswan Dam in retaliation. "No," said a heavy-set Israeli with black, curly hair, "we would never do that. That would be a strike against civilians."

The lights flickered on and off. An American reporter went to the stairway leading up into the press building. The cannon booms were louder. An army girl with long brown hair and dark eyes was sitting partway up the staircase. Her face was pale. The reporter smiled. "Don't be afraid," he said in English. The girl raised her eyes to him and tried to smile in return. She shook her head and looked back down at the stairs. They were both afraid, and the sharing of fear is a form of momentary love.

The undulating sound of the second siren pealed through the press building. Someone came down the stairs shouting "All clear!" in Hebrew and English. Everybody went back up to the entrance hall and out into the cool darkness. There are no flies in Israel, and Heaven appears to be closer to earth there than it does in Egypt. A map of stars hung above the city, shimmering like a bed of luminous diamond particles seen through shallow, clear water. People were sitting on the steps of the press building. Off to the east the dark horizon was periodically lit up by spreading orange flashes. The boom of cannon followed the flashes. Two rips of fire jagged almost simultaneously, and the twin thumps of sound were heard as an explosive stutter. The Israelis were in an artillery duel with the Jordanian batteries outside the city of Qalqilya. A famous British correspondent appeared on the steps. By the dim blue light of the press-building hall, his face was spoiled and serene. Someone complimented him on a book he had written about China years before. The spoiled face smiled. "My dear fellow," he murmured, "my dear, dear fellow." He was quite drunk.

A woman said she saw a "shell" coming over the city during the air alert. Had she seen a rocket? No one knew. Somebody else said he had just talked to an Israeli editor who had come from the special briefing. Israel, the editor was quoted as having said, had won a "fantastic victory"—it was the second time that evocative phrase had been used in the vacuum of information. More than 300 Egyptian and Syrian aircraft had been destroyed on the ground, it was said the editor had said. Three flashes spread in quick succession across the eastern horizon and three booms rattled through the darkness. The night was soft and cool, and, for the first time that day, the people who watched on the steps began to relax. With its square structures silhouetted against the bed of stars, Tel Aviv was suddenly beautiful and seemed to be holding itself in the dark, proud posture of survival.

The correspondents were called upstairs to the briefing hall. Colonel Pearlman's press conference would be held at 9:45, said a tall, muscular officer. Meanwhile some minor bits of information might be useful. The Americans had announced in Washington that they were "neutral in thought, word and deed." The major grinned and the Israeli correspondents in the hall guffawed. When the laughter died down, it was

announced that Austrian Airlines would try a flight
from Tel Aviv to Europe that night and any television
correspondents who wanted to get film out had better
take it to the airport immediately.

The major said that the Jordanians had begun shelling an area fifteen kilometers north of Tel Aviv at 7:30.
By 8:05 Natanya had come under fire for the second
time that day. At 8:20 Jordanian fire began hitting the
area around the airport at Lydda.

In Jerusalem, Prime Minister Eshkol met with the
Knesset toward the middle of the evening. As Israeli
and Jordanian forces barreled mortar shells at each
other with street-shaking crashes only a few blocks
away, the parliamentarians held a celebration in the
blacked-out anteroom of their chamber. There was
more exhilarated profanity than thankful prayer. "People say that Israel is like Czechoslovakia," said one
Knesset member to a reporter. "Well, you tell them
that Hitler may have screwed Czechoslovakia, but we're
going to screw Nasser."

As explosions shook the building all around them,
the Knesset sat in the darkness and listened to the
Prime Minister's report. Three Arab air forces had been
almost totally destroyed. Three armored columns were
blasting their way west across the Sinai, engaging the
Egyptians in ferocious night battles—for which the Israelis are excellently trained and for which the Arabs
are trained hardly at all. Heavy artillery fire was crossing the Jordanian and Syrian borders, but those two
Arab armies had not advanced.

The Knesset members knew it all already—Jerusalem has one of the most fruitful grapevines of any capital anywhere—but they cheered themselves into exhaustion. There was a jubilant foresight in the chamber
that this was going to be even better than 1956.

Back at the press center in Tel Aviv, 10:15 came and went and Colonel Pearlman's briefing was postponed once more. The correspondents were getting restless and irritated. The tough, good-natured major put a crude map into a slide projector and re-described the day's pattern of shelling, bombing and flat trajectory fire upon Israel from Rosh Pinna in the north to the southern sectors of Jerusalem. He added that some of the Jordanian shells had hit central Tel Aviv in the area of Masaryk Square an hour before.

Again a group of correspondents set off by foot in the blackout to see the damage. All around them they could feel, hear, but not see the life of the city. People coughed and murmured in the deep gloom; occasionally a body would brush past—but the streets were almost empty.

In the dim beams of a flashlight flicked on quickly and switched off, the reporters saw a little old man walking his dog. He had a soft, bushy wave of white hair in the Ben-Gurion style and wore a sport shirt with an open collar. Did he speak English? Yes, a little. Did he know Masaryk Square? Yes, he would lead them. The group set off again. They walked in silence for a few blocks and then one of the correspondents asked the old man what he thought of the war.

"Well," replied the soft, accent-cluttered voice, "they do say there will be one."

"But it began today!"

"Is that so?"

"Of course! Haven't you heard?"

"My, my. Are we winning?"

"You are indeed. It's fantastic!"

"You don't say? Well, well."

"That's why the streets are blacked out," a reporter said.

"Yes," the old man answered, "they told me there was a blackout tonight, but they didn't tell me why."

He was blind.

In the open area around Masaryk Square the reporters could see, by starlight, a group of men standing in the street talking softly among themselves. No one knew anything about buildings in that district being hit. "If it came in around here, it must have been a very small, soft shell," one of the men said. They all laughed. "Is it the Jordanians?"

Someone said it was.

"Those bastards."

The men all laughed again.

Back at the press center the briefing hall was full. Correspondents and officers moved up and down the aisles, chatting and complaining about the delay. Crises are the conventions of journalism. Old friends from opposite sides of the world meet and update each other on their fortunes. Old events are reviewed and old wars are re-fought. That night the two earlier Arab-Israeli wars had been thoroughly hashed over by midnight. By then even the pleasures of exaggerated retrospection had lost their charm and the reporters were all thoroughly cross by the time Colonel Pearlman finally appeared at forty minutes after midnight.

The chief spokesman of the Israeli defense ministry—he had been spokesman in the 1948 and 1956 wars, too—is the true personification of a curious Israeli type, the British-born Jewish officer who appears to be more British than Jewish. Britain is perhaps the only contemporary nation whose culture is so attractive that even her former enemies pay her the compliment of imitating British styles in speech, dress, mannerism and military tactics. Colonel Pearlman is a slight man with a bristling military mustache and the nervous wit of the senior common room. "Sorry to have kept you all waiting," he said, "but my masters would have torn strips off me if I'd come along any sooner." He smiled a lumpy smile and put on his steel-framed glasses. "I am now prepared to read out reports from the various commanders." He looked up and smiled again. "Here is the position as of now."

Then, at last, the world found out what had happened on the first day of the third Arab-Israeli war.

Colonel Pearlman turned to the Sinai first. In the northern sector the Israelis had captured Khan Yunis, Rafah, Sheik Zuweib and El Arish. One column was headed out of El Arish toward Abu Agwila while another was fighting on the outskirts of Gaza. The names, at that stage, meant very little to the foreign correspondents; they had studied the maps during the day, but the alien labels didn't fit specific places except for Gaza and El Arish. But the foreigners could tell from the gasps and murmurs of their Israeli colleagues that what Colonel Pearlman was saying was marvelous.

In the central desert the bases of Auja Hafir and Tarah Umm had been taken and there was bitter fighting raging inside the Egyptian defensive positions at Umm Katef. In the south the Israeli tanks had burst out of Kuntilla and had captured a good number of enemy forward positions. He reviewed the artillery duels along the Jordanian and Syrian fronts and repeated the statement that Tel Aviv had been hit.

Colonel Pearlman took off his glasses. "Now, as to the day's air activity, I shall read out the report of General Mordecai Hod, the commander of our air force."

The glasses went back on and the thin face frowned upon a messy batch of papers in the colonel's hands. "As you undoubtedly already know, we have confronted the air forces of Egypt, Syria and Jordan and Iraq to-day." He paused, raised his head and looked out over the hall full of silent, expectant correspondents. "In that confrontation," said Colonel Pearlman, "we destroyed 374 enemy aircraft."

The tense hush exploded in a roar of shouting and applause.

"Those are the figures—"

The clapping and cheering drowned out the colonel's words. He waited. The noise subsided.

"Those are the figures of certainty," Pearlman said. "There are also 34 probables—"

An officer stepped up onto the platform and whispered something. Colonel Pearlman nodded.

"I have just been informed that the final statement is being held up," he said. "Perhaps we can confirm some of the probables for you."

But it didn't really matter. Everyone in the room knew that the war had been won and all that remained was to follow the dark angel's shadow to the edge of the warrior's world.

And war is a sleepless trade.

As Colonel Pearlman was telling the first public truths about the battle in the first hours of Tuesday, June 6, Israeli jets were howling low over the Jordanian capital of Amman and Israeli artillery was blasting at Jordanian positions around Jerusalem. With the Egyptians stunned and fighting for their lives in the Sinai, the Israelis had begun to turn their metallic wrath upon the Hashemite Kingdom of Hussein. Tracers and shells cut the darkness into fiery ribbons and Israeli troops began their invasion of Jordan by taking Latrun on the southwest bulge of the West Bank before the sun was fully up. The encirclement of Jerusalem began and orders went out to commanders to direct their fire away from the holy places in the Old City. That day more than 500 civilians were injured on the Israeli side of Jerusalem as the fire-fights grew more intense.

At 3:20 a.m. the first sounds of desperation began to come from Cairo. It is an interesting measure of the Arab capacity to live so completely on the two separate planes of verbal and physical reality that the Egyptians could, before dawn on Tuesday, proclaim victory and beseech their allies to save them from defeat. At 3:20 Cairo Radio appealed to its "brothers in Syria—army and people. Advance across the borders! The army of Jordan has liberated parts of the usurped land! The army of Iraq has penetrated the occupied land, crushing the enemy positions! The army of Egypt has been storming the Zionist concentrations in the Negev! So, brothers in Syria, advance across the borders. Advance and strike the enemy! Advance and destroy its existence! Liberate Palestine with us! The day is yours! You have lived and worked for this day! You have indeed helped in making it a day of revenge, a day of return, a day on which the Israeli gang disappears from all of Palestine. . . ."

Glowering and flinging down artillery shells from the Heights of Golan above the Israeli plain, the Syrians heard but did not move. Perhaps something profoundly Arabic in their characters leaped the chasm between hope and truth to create doubt that Israel was, at that hour, going down for the third time under the combined, victorious assaults of the Jordanians, Egyptians and Iraqis. Or perhaps the Syrians had been listening to the Jerusalem radio reports of Colonel Pearlman's briefing. At any rate, they never did move, and in the end the Israelis had to climb the heights to give the Syrians their war.

In Cairo the problem was not one of attempting to bridge the gap between hope and truth but, rather, of having it forcibly bridged by the air damage and the reports from the commanders in the Sinai. For the first twelve hours of the war the Egyptian combat reportage had been illusory. Then some—but not all—of the field officers were forced to admit that things were bad; they began to call for help, especially air cover. In Amman, King Hussein also clung to the hope that the Egyptians were holding the bulk of their aircraft in reserve for a massive counterstrike upon Israel. At 4:50 a.m. President Nasser put through a call to King Hussein. This was the famous conversation in which the Big Lie of American and British intervention on the side of Israel was cooked up. The Israelis monitored and tape-recorded the call—not an especially difficult thing to do since telephone connections between Cairo and Amman are on radio circuits and the bands are well known. There are many puzzling things about this particular telephone call and certainly one of them is why the two Arab leaders concocted such foolishness on a telephone circuit that they must have known would be monitored.

Another puzzling aspect is the erratic nature of the conversation as the Israelis published it. We hear aides of the two leaders making the connection and summoning their masters. Then:

> NASSER: How are you? I hear His Majesty, the brother, wants to know if the fighting is going on along all the front?
> HUSSEIN: Yes. Shall we include also the U.S.? Do you know of this, shall we announce that the U.S. is co-operating with Israel?

Obviously something has been left out here between Nasser's first statement and Hussein's reply. Or the two leaders had conferred earlier and had, during that prior conversation, come up with the basic story. Hussein's statement doesn't follow on Nasser's—even if the peculiarities of the Arabic language are taken into consideration.

The two Arab leaders then agree that they will announce that Britain and the United States are both in league with Israel. Toward the end of the conversation Nasser appears to be misleading Hussein.

NASSER: A thousand thanks, don't give up, we are with you with all our heart and we are flying our planes over Israel today, our planes are striking at Israel's airfields since morning.

Perhaps, like the earlier appeal to the Syrians, this was an attempt to goad the Jordanians into attacking across the border into Israel.

In the monitored telephone conversation Hussein appears to be participating in the creation of a falsehood. Yet there is considerable evidence to demonstrate that at one point he probably believed that planes from the American Sixth Fleet, cruising in the eastern Mediterranean, had in fact attacked Egypt.

On Monday the Jordanian monitoring station at Ajlun behind the Judean range had picked up on its radarscopes the images of aircraft hurtling in from the Mediterranean to hit Egypt. Because of its particular location behind mountains nearly 3,000 feet high, the Ajlun station cannot spot aircraft flying low out of Israel. Nothing closer than fifty miles from the Israeli coast is visible on the station's Marconi-247 gear. Thus, the Jordanians may have really believed that the low-flying Israeli fighter-bombers which suddenly appeared on their scopes were in fact British and American aircraft attacking Egypt. If that is the case, one wonders

why King Hussein, in the early hours of Tuesday morning, agreed to lie about something he thought was true.
Perhaps the poor young man didn't know what President Nasser was talking about and just decided to go
along for the ride.

At 6:45 a.m. Cairo Radio announced that "it has
been conclusively proved that a large-scale assistance
is rendered to Israel by U.S. and British aircraft carriers."

Such is the redemptory balm of the rationalizing
word that this story was repeated, magnified, woven
into Arab diplomacy and, finally, became official history. It had an irritating effect on the Russians, who on
Wednesday called in the Arab ambassadors in Moscow,
including Murad Galeb of Egypt, and asked some
pointed questions: why hadn't the radar of the Russian
fleet shadowing the Americans in the eastern Mediterranean picked up signs of the alleged American attack
on Egypt? And how could the British have participated
in carrier-based raids when their carriers were 1,500
miles away? It is not certain who conducted this interview on the Soviet side. But, whoever he was, he blew
up at the end of the conversation, accused the Arabs of
trying to start World War III and told them to cut it
the hell out.

A little after six o'clock on Tuesday morning an
Iraqi Tupelov-16 bomber roared across the Jordanian
border at Israel's narrowest point and splattered the
coastal city of Natanya with bombs. A Mirage III rose
from the north. The Tupelov did a wing-wrenching turn
over Natanya and streaked back for Jordan with the
Mirage III hot on its tail. There was a white flash, a
roar, and bits of the Tupelov flew all over the eastern
sky.

A flight of Israeli fighter-bombers tore off toward

Iraq and rocketed and bombed the airfield H-3, from which the Tupelov had come.

Early that morning also, the Israelis broke into Jordan at the curious little hump of the West Bank which protrudes into Israel northwest of Jerusalem. They captured the town of Latrun. In the north the town of Jenin was encircled by a complex series of maneuvers that had begun the night before. The Israelis now had footholds on the south-central West Bank and on its northern corner. The two forces began to fight their way toward each other along the mountains of Judea— that range so formidable that Napoleon had refused to march through it. The warriors were coming home; from that range their tribal ancestors of the Kingdoms of Judah and Israel had commanded the world.

In the burning noon of Tuesday four correspondents drove up to Natanya to see the damage. At the police station a German-speaking officer said that the raid had killed one woman and injured twenty-six people. The Tupelov had approached so quickly that the air-raid alarm was late in going off. A woman had gone out onto her balcony to see what was happening and the house had taken a direct hit.

For three blocks down the main street of low buildings every window had been blown out. Two of the scatter-bombs had ripped into an apartment building with a radio shop on its first floor. The shop was a shambles of gaping concrete holes, bent steel girders and rubble. A friend of the owner stood in the mess. "It isn't so terrible," he said to the reporters. "We'll make them pay for it." He laughed, blinked and scratched his chin.

All up and down the main street, Herzl Avenue, people were sweeping glass into piles and hauling away the movable pieces of broken junk with their bare hands. They seemed almost proud of the two days of shelling and bombing Natanya had taken. They laughed, chattered and vied with each other in pointing out the worst bits—a burned automobile, an apartment with all of its windows blown out and the slats of venetian blinds hanging like ribs detached from a spine, the blank forty-foot-high wall of a bank building that had been punctured in one clean hole by a flying bomb. There was a sense in the town that came close to exhilaration, a relief, perhaps, that had transformed itself into defiant eagerness to see what the next raid or shelling would bring. Israel is a nation of professional survivors and their descendants. The national characteristics of toughness and a love of taking risks—sometimes wildly foolish ones—seem to come from some deep need; perhaps it is as simple as the need to rebut the centuries-old prototype of the outnumbered, persecuted Jew of Europe wailing, beating his breast and imploring man and God to witness his latest suffering at the hands of the goyim.

The cult of unflinchableness is also national in dimension. The correspondents left Natanya and drove east toward the Jordanian border and the mountain village of Tulkarm just beyond Israeli territory. The road leading east from Natanya is one of the strategic routes of Israel. From coast to border it is only twelve miles long. If—as the Arabs had planned—Israel was to be cut in three pieces, it was along this road that the Jordanians would invade while the Egyptians sliced off the Negev in the south.

It was a hushed, bee-humming summer afternoon. A dozen Israeli soldiers had made a camp in a lemon grove four miles along the road toward the border. Lying propped on their packs, they waved gaily as the correspondents drove past.

Ten miles off to the south, Long Toms boomed in the bright sunlight. The Israelis were mounting their final attack on Qalqilya, the city from which the Jordanians had shelled Lydda and Tel Aviv the night before. Super-Mystères glinted in the afternoon sun as they streaked in from the northwest toward Qalqilya. High, high above them against the blue dome of the sky an Iraqi MIG-21 wheeled like an indecisive bird of prey.

The road led past a kibbutz where children played before a barracks-like building and an old man pottered in his garden—all of them oblivious to the distant sounds and close, flying sights of war. They were being unflinchable.

Suddenly, a mile or so from the border, the correspondents realized that their bright blue car was the only moving target in the area. They stopped. In the distance ahead of them Tulkarm was spread over the top of a hill; it is an ancient Arab town of square gray buildings that cluster low on the slopes and crest of the rise.

In the halcyon setting of summer framed by the motionless enemy landscape ahead and the thuds and screeches of war in the distance, the correspondents suddenly felt alone and scared. They turned the car around and raced back up the road, past the old man and the children, past the waving troops and back to the road for Tel Aviv.

That evening Colonel Pearlman recapitulated the story of the day; it was a variation on the theme of Monday. In the desert, where the main energies of combat were being expended, the focus was Abu Agwila, one corner of a roaring, flaming triangle into which the Egyptian armor was being driven. Since morning the Israelis had knocked out or captured 150 tanks. A violent armored battle—perhaps the last one in history unless the Arabs would be indiscreet enough to try this sort of warfare with the Israelis again—was taking place in the north-central Sinai. It would continue all through the night and into the next day; tanks were burning in the triangle and there had been, said Colonel Pearlman, "some very grim action." The Egyptians on all three Sinai fronts seemed to be withdrawing toward the hills in the west—which was exactly what the Israelis wanted. The only way through the hills was the Mitla Pass, which was going to become world famous as the graveyard of Egyptian armor. The second line seemed to have disappeared from its stationary positions in the west. Some of the units had driven forward to meet the Israelis and were now being herded into the triangle. Others, realizing what was happening farther to the east, had fled. There had been air battles over the Sinai as the Egyptians expended their surviving stock of flying machinery in a desperate attempt to mop back the flood of battle streaming toward the Delta. Two MIG-21's and six Sukhois had been blasted out of the sky.

On the Jordanian front, artillery had been bombarding villages and settlements from Rosh Pinna in the north to the southern suburbs of Jerusalem. More than one hundred houses had been hit and a violent battle was going on as the Israelis prepared to storm the gates of the Old City in the most dramatic and controversial acquisition of territory in the whole war. Qalqilya had been taken in the late afternoon and there would be no shelling of Tel Aviv and Lydda that night. The great pincer was moving its arms together with the Jordanian West Bank between them; its hinges were Jenin in the north and Latrun in the south. The Syrians had mounted an attack of sorts and had been driven back. They were glowering on Golan again and hurtling artillery shells down upon settlements and farms.

That day the Israelis opened another front. Abba Eban had left for the United Nations in New York. At the airport he had said, "The change in relationships which will come about after this fighting should ensure conditions which will enable the citizens of Israel to live in peace and quiet."

That seemed fair and logical enough. But it was false prophecy. By her victories, Israel angered and frightened her friends. She also succeeded in widening the gulf between the American government and the American people. In the confusing darkness of their own condition, the Americans watched the simplistic and comprehensible violence of the third Arab-Israeli war, first with anxiety and then with exultation as the battle surged in a sunblaze of glory toward the Israeli victory. This sort of triumph added an element of shame to the various loathings that Americans had for their own government's conduct in Vietnam. To the hawks of Washington the Dayanesque militance and savage expertise of the Israelis seemed an obvious object lesson for U.S. commanders and strategists in Vietnam (a point of view based on the mistaken assumption that the two wars were strategically comparable). To American doubters of the dove variety—especially those who opposed the Southeast Asian war on moral grounds— Israel's victory in the first week of June 1967 answered the question that had tormented American moralists for years: if all wars are immoral but some wars are necessary, how do you define necessity? Israel had produced an answer that anyone who wanted to understand could. Nations have an obligation to keep themselves from being obliterated, and this is a higher morality than abstinence from violence. If Arab grievance and hatred were to be taken at their face value, not much imagination was needed to conceive of what would have happened to Israel if the Arabs had overwhelmed her. No one had seriously argued that South Vietnam would culturally and physically cease to be if the communists absorbed it. The difference between the two threats was reflected in the attitudes of the two threatened peoples to the wars they were fighting. Every Israeli was enthusiastic about having a go at the Arabs—except for a few who objected on religious grounds. Among the South Vietnamese army and people there was a noticeable indifference to fighting the Viet Cong or the armies of North Vietnam. Israel did not require a great outside power to explain to her what her war was all about or to prod her into action.

National viewpoints are arrived at by a complex and tormented process; they are influenced by geography, history and immediate obsession. Israel's geography is modest and her history is long, emotive and not entirely evident because it has to do with much more than the country itself. In the diplomacy of the third Arab-Israeli war the misunderstandings grew large, raw and nerve-racking. Their symbol was Jerusalem. On the question of its capture and unification by force, Israel's friends in the West took the exterior view; they saw the question of Jerusalem in the perspective of larger implications that ranged from a political re-settlement of the Middle East to the irritation points of the cold war. The great Western powers understood that Jerusalem had a special importance for the Israelis, but they didn't understand the depth of that importance or the reasoning that lay behind it—at least they didn't understand with the same passionate subjectivity that is involved in the larger process of being an Israeli Jew. On their side, the Israelis understood the exterior implications of the Jerusalem question. It was explained to them over and over again by American and British diplomats. But even if they had wanted to, the Israelis could not have accommodated the exterior implications of the issues because those implications simply could not be squared with everything that had gone before—all the pain, glory, suffering and contradiction that had molded the character of the Jews of Israel.

In a tragic way the misunderstandings between Israel and her greatest friends in the world became a classic dialogue of the diplomatic deaf where, before the war, it was a struggle of good intentions against the tendency of tragedy to be fulfilled.

The machinery with which history moves toward its tragedies is made of unrelated and disparate parts operating independently of each other, yet directed toward a common end. In this case the parts of the machinery were the individual characters of certain men—Nasser, the flawed Arab; Dayan, the warrior whose decision that war was inevitable had been arrived at while Levi Eshkol, the Russian-born Prime Minister, was still searching for an alternative; Hussein, the simplistic king cursed with a penchant for either/or; and Lyndon B. Johnson, carrying an insupportable burden of earnest hope. The other parts of the historic tragedy's machinery were the general natures of two complicated peoples— the land-rich Arabs searching for unity and the homogeneous Jews defending a dream of land come true.

These and perhaps half a dozen other factors developing in their separate compartments on the historic landscape worked together to create the momentum that led to war. Since their relationship to each other was only in the end they achieved, the total working of the machinery's various parts could not be halted. Therefore the end was inevitable.

When cool, Israel is a microcosm of every sort of political sentiment imaginable; its right-wingers have the same nationalistic self-righteousness as right-wingers in America, Britain and France. Its communist party is as marooned in doctrinaire isolation from the twentieth century as any other. In its cool periods Israel tends to throw up governments that are created out of its political center—Mapai, the most conservative of the three Israeli labor parties. Mapai is also the center of the Israeli political establishment. It has the comfy stability of the British Labor Party.

But when it grows hot, Israel demands a government that expresses something more than orthodox political plans and ideas. During the heated periods Israel conceives of action as the primary function of government. The pressure which makes Israel hot had been growing for two years as the El Assifa terrorist raids increased in volume and sophistication.

Yet the effect of mounting heat in Israel is not so simple as public belligerence. Rather, a nervous sense about time develops and the demand for action crystallizes out of several understandable factors. The Israelis dislike being pushed about by people whom they have proved are weaker than themselves, they develop a mordant sense of déjà vu as the symptoms of crisis mount, and they begin to search for leaders who will express the public mood with clarity. When the heat becomes extreme, the political complexion of the country undergoes a complete change. If the center continues to be too compromising and comfy, the Israelis become unhappy with it. The demand is first for some sort of self-reasserting action. Then, at the point where the factors converge and war is assumed to be unavoidable, those who are for any solution short of war are judged to be men dithering in the face of unpleasant reality.

In the spring of 1967 Israel had the comfiest government in its history. Levi Eshkol, the Prime Minister, was a man whose character was rooted in the toughness of the first-generation returnee, one who could still remember the pogroms of Russia. But his genius was for compromise—an art which is indispensable to the operation of coalition politics and one which Eshkol conducted with nice Yiddish humor and an extreme sensitivity to the moods of other people. His principal Cabinet officers—the inner Cabinet—were Abba Eban and Yigal Allon, a leading figure in Achdut Ha'avoda, another of the labor parties which was in the coalition with Mapai, the National Religious Party, the left-wing Mapam and one other group. Allon had been a brilliant leader of the anti-British underground and a hero of the 1948 war. He was no militant, however. He had once said, "For Israel, to avert a war is much more important than to win it."

But the establishment was split. A complex excursion through the lower depths of power known as the Lavon affair had created a deep and bitter rift between Eshkol and his old chief, David Ben-Gurion, the former Premier. Ben-Gurion had taken a few colleagues into the wilderness—Moshe Dayan included—to form Rafi. It is, perhaps, the only political party anywhere with an old man's disgruntlement as its charter.

It was upon a divided Israeli establishment and the publicly uninspiring but competent Eshkol government that the 1967 crisis devolved. The countdown started with Nasser's move into the Sinai Desert on May 14.

At this point Eshkol began his battle on two fronts. He was as determined as anyone else that the Arabs should not fall into the illusion that Israel was backing off from their threats. But his differences with Rafi, with the Israeli hawks and, eventually, with public opinion itself were over timing and the question of when the moment had come at which several options were reduced to two.

For the benefit of his opponents at home as much as for the edification of the Arabs, Eshkol had been putting on displays of public severity. On May 13 he had denounced Syria as the real progenitor of the crisis. "We shall choose the time, the place and the means to counter the aggressor," he warned.

On May 15—Israeli Independence Day—there had been a military parade in Jerusalem; this made the major Western powers nervous and unhappy. They didn't recognize the divided, controversial city as Israel's capital and thought that the parade would further inflame an already jittery situation.

Egyptian troops continued to pour into the desert; the bombast from Cairo, Damascus, Baghdad and Amman grew more raucous; the tempo of terrorist raids grew quicker; and the uneasy heat of public opinion began to infect the military. They warned the Prime Minister that, for every day he delayed taking action, he was adding 200 military casualties to the price Israel would eventually pay in war.

The public demands upon Mr. Eshkol were not so much for war at that stage as they were for a whacking good retaliation raid similar to the one he had ordered against Es Sammu in Jordan the previous November. But the Cabinet felt that a retaliation raid would, at such a precarious moment, detonate the whole Middle East. It was especially leery of hitting Syria; there was a feeling in the Cabinet that the Soviets had invested their main hopes for the area in the neurotic government of Nourredin El Atassi and that the Russians could be provoked into defending it with force.

The hawks, the military and Rafi had come to the

conclusion that the choice was narrowing to a stark selection between fight or surrender. Public opinion was moving in the same direction but hadn't got there yet. Only one more act of Arab belligerence—even a small one—was needed, however, to persuade even the Israeli public that war was inevitable and that he who hung back was dithering.

The belligerent act was not small. It was at this highly combustible stage of developments that Nasser seized the Gulf of Aqaba.

The gulf is more than an economic necessity to Israel. It is a highly emotive symbol. The Israeli nation was born in conflict and conducted its adolescence in a nursery of encirclement. Until 1956 the psychology of Israel toward her Arab neighbors was the psychology of a besieged wagon train toward the Indians. The 1956 war—conducted with British and French help—produced a change in the Israeli psychology even though it was a victory of combat that turned into a diplomatic defeat. Aside from stopping terrorist raids upon herself, the only thing that Israel had really won when the long post-war haggling was finished was one break in the circle around her: the Gulf of Aqaba had been opened. There was a window in the stifling nursery. The United Nations took over the fortress of Sharm El Sheik, and it was now possible for oil tankers to sail up to the port of Eilat and for Israeli trade with Africa and Asia to develop. The United States had promised that if Aqaba were ever closed, it would move to reopen the waterway.

Above everything else, the Gulf of Aqaba was a symbol that the 1956 war had been fought for reasons more solid than teaching the Arabs the lesson that Israel must be left alone.

The events since May 14 had demonstrated that the Arabs hadn't learned the lesson. The terrorist raids had

resumed again. With Nasser's seizure of the Gulf of
Aqaba, the last and largest prize won with so much
blood and anxiety had been taken away. And it was
then that the third Arab-Israeli war became inevitable
even though it was eventually fought for different reasons.

Yet when such a moment arrives only a unified nation acts upon its truth. Israel was not unified. Eshkol
and the hawks—who included Moshe Dayan—were
still in disagreement over the question of whether the
moment for war *had* arrived. Paradoxically, David Ben-
Gurion, the man who had presided over the victory of
1956, was to sink deeper and deeper into doubt as the
actual fighting approached. Mr. Ben-Gurion was a
prisoner of the history he had helped to create; in 1956
Israel had gone to war in the company of Britain and
France. For various strategic and political reasons
David Ben-Gurion came to doubt the wisdom of going
alone this time. He also thought that the timing had got
out of kilter when May 23 passed with no immediate
military reaction to Nasser.

To some degree—but with different results—this was
the attitude of Abba Eban, too. During the events of
1956 he had been the Israeli ambassador in Washington
and at the United Nations. As such, he had been the
lightning rod for all the threats and demands flung at
Israel by President Eisenhower and Secretary Dulles.
To have both the United States and the Soviet Union
denouncing you when you are fighting a war that you
consider essential to your vital interests can, obviously,
be an upsetting experience.

Eban's traumatized condition added to Premier Eshkol's instinct for compromise and Yigal Allon's belief
that the avoidance of war is a higher glory than victory.
The Cabinet was still dominated by Mapai, Achdut

Ha'avoda and the National Religious Party—none of them combative by philosophy and all of them anxious to avoid a military showdown if it was at all possible.

If the choices had narrowed, there was still one big alternative to the poles of fight or surrender: see what Israel's allies—mainly the United States—intended to do.

On May 24 Mr. Eban flew to Paris and talked to General de Gaulle for forty-five minutes. The President of France complimented the foreign minister of Israel on his excellent command of the French language and suggested that Israel not shoot first. General de Gaulle was keeping his own options flexible.

In London the Prime Minister of the world's oldest maritime nation told Mr. Eban that keeping the Gulf of Aqaba open was a Good Thing and Britain was determined that it should be done. Abba Eban felt mildly encouraged.

On May 25 he flew to Washington.

The role that the Americans played in the diplomatic prelude to the third Arab-Israeli war is the subject of a good deal of private and public controversy. It is said, among other things, that the United States could have done more. But, in terms of the possibilities and the American condition, this is unfair. Lord Acton was wrong; power—at least supreme power—doesn't corrupt. It creates anguish, uncertainty and a self-distrust that result in supreme caution. The dilemma of powerful nations is incapable of solution. They are in a constant whipsaw, either being denounced for acting in a way that their power makes seem belligerent, or being summoned to action by their weaker friends.

The Americans, in the summer of 1967, were deep in the Vietnam bog, and the national atmosphere was one of dark, fretful mush. In the midst of all of this, the United States agreed that it had made a promise to Israel concerning the Gulf of Aqaba ten years before and it intended to keep the promise. But the matter wasn't that simple. Even before Eban arrived in Washington the Johnson administration had been sending messages all over the Middle East, to Moscow and to Western Europe. At the United Nations, Ambassador Goldberg had tried to get the Security Council to pass a resolution urging President Nasser to be cautious. This had been frustrated by the Soviets. When Abba Eban got off the plane at Washington's National Airport he told reporters that he had come to find out what the United States was going to do about the mounting peril to Israel.

This immediately irritated President Johnson. He had been harped at for years about the uses of power and didn't need any more harping from the Israelis. The United States had four choices of action. It could —theoretically, anyway—use force to open the Strait of Tiran and the Gulf of Aqaba. Or it could act in concert with other nations, trying persuasion first and then multi-national force later, if necessary. There was always the possibility of just looking the other way while the Israelis opened the strait themselves. Or—finally— the Americans could resort to a complex diplomatic formula that would throw the whole issue into the International Court of Justice at The Hague.

The second choice—multi-lateral persuasion and then force if necessary—was the only practical and palatable one, and the preparation of such a plan was already in train as Mr. Eban drove off to the Israeli embassy on Twenty-second Street.

He was due to see Secretary Rusk at 5:30 p.m. Alarmed cables were coming into the embassy from Jerusalem. Israeli intelligence had picked up signs that an Egyptian attack was about to begin; Prime Minister Eshkol said that his chief of intelligence would stake his reputation on it. Eban had someone telephone the State Department to say that he must see Secretary Rusk at once. At four o'clock he was escorted to the seventh floor of the department. The Israeli foreign minister was tense and agitated. His hands were trembling and he kept touching his face in a nervous gesture. He told American officials about the cables from Tel Aviv. Members of Dean Rusk's secretariat called the Central Intelligence Agency, which said, on a first-reaction basis only, that it had seen no indication of an impending Egyptian attack.

While the CIA worked through the night re-assessing the situation, Undersecretary Rostow and a group of senior State Department officials explained to Abba Eban and his aides the plan that the United States was working on. First, a group of major maritime nations would sign a declaration on the right of innocent passage through the Gulf of Aqaba. This declaration, it was hoped, would have impressive signatory power if not actual clout. It would be a test of whether the Egyptians were susceptible to diplomatic pressure. If not, there was the possibility that an international naval force could be put together to open the Strait of Tiran. It was a long evening at the State Department.

The next morning the Central Intelligence Agency reported that it could still find no evidence that the Egyptians were about to attack Israel. Later in the morning the Egyptian ambassador in Washington was summoned to the State Department and questioned. He claimed to know nothing about an attack. Still later on the morning of May 26 the Americans received a strong message from the Soviet government repeating the bizarre charge of May 13—that an Israeli attack on Egypt was im-

minent. Patiently the Americans questioned Eban, and
wearily Eban replied, for perhaps the twentieth time,
that it simply wasn't true. The United States sent two
cables back to Moscow saying that it doubted the alle-
gation.

The confusion deepened. Abba Eban went to see Secretary of Defense McNamara and then returned to the
Israeli embassy to prepare for a midday appointment
with President Johnson. The time of the appointment
came and went. The White House said it wasn't ready.
Later in the afternoon Ephraim Evron, the Israeli minister in Washington, went to the Executive Mansion to
arrange a new time. To his astonishment, he was suddenly whisked into the President's office, where Mr.
Johnson threw a verbal hammerlock on him. For an
hour the President talked steadily to the astonished minister, explaining all the things that the United States was
trying to do for Israel. Though Mr. Evron was not specifically prepared and though he was outranked by his
ambassador and the foreign minister, he tried, from
time to time, to explain the anxieties in Jerusalem and
the deteriorating political situation inside Israel at large.
It was an uphill run and Ephraim Evron was still listening and trying to get a word in edgewise when Abba
Eban and Ambassador Avraham Harmon arrived at the
wrong White House gate. There were a few moments of
turmoil during which the people outside the Executive
Mansion tried to get in and the people inside tried to
locate those outside. Finally a guard telephoned that
some guy named Eban was at the gate claiming that he
had an appointment with the President.

Once everybody was sorted out, Mr. Johnson began
again. Though he cloaked his declarations in Texas rhetoric ("we want to see that li'l ole blue and white Israeli
flag sailin' up the Gulf of Aqaba"), the President was

serious. He went over the two-phased plan again. The British and the Canadians, who had originally been enthusiastic about participating in the American scheme (it was, as a matter of fact, British in origin), were now cooling off and only the Dutch were still committed. If an international force could not be assembled and if the maritime declaration failed, said Mr. Johnson, the United States would act by itself to open the Gulf of Aqaba. The President warned, however, that he needed more time.

For all of his upcountry jargon and patriotic platitudes, President Johnson is quite a persuasive man in private and the evening of May 26 was apparently one of his best efforts. It must have been, because it postponed the war for ten days. On the face of it, the American plan was a modest and nebulous effort, especially when placed against the evident peril and the overheated tensions in Israel. This is not to say that it was a bad plan—it was probably the best one possible. And the administration was desperately serious about it. In the glory of their good intentions the Americans didn't realize that the time for diplomacy had almost run out. The last bit did run out while they were still trying.

Even the logic with which the United States government gently rebuffed the anxious Israeli requests for military reassurance was built of the stuff from which eggshells are made. At both the State Department and the White House Mr. Eban was told that, under the United States Constitution, the President could not go to war without the approval of Congress. With nary a glance toward Vietnam, the Israeli foreign minister—who knew all about the Constitution anyway—accepted this. It would, perhaps, have been rude and futile to do otherwise. What the administration was really saying was that Congress wouldn't stand for two wars. There

had been interesting sounds from some of the Capitol
Hill hawks who said that if it ever came down to a
choice it would be a far, far better thing to defend Israel
than to continue the sordid and interminable adventure
in Vietnam. The question, however, was strictly aca-
demic. Vietnam had priority.

On Saturday Mr. Eban flew home to Israel.

Within the Cabinet and beyond it, the atmosphere
had grown heavier and the issue had shifted from Aqaba
to the threatening Arab military build-up on all sides.
The terrorist raids were getting worse, and the sounds
of ferocity had assumed a strident vulgarity. But it was
the Egyptian deployment in the Sinai which had become
the focal point of all plans and arguments. There were
seven divisions and 900 tanks implanted fifty miles deep
in the desert opposite Israel's southern borders. Israeli
reconnaissance flights had photographed the two-bank
Soviet-style arrangement. To the chiefs of staff, this was
hardly a feint or a political exercise. The press was growing critical, especially of the fact that the Prime Minister
still held the defense portfolio. In times of duress, lov-
able-uncle types do not inspire confidence as defense
ministers. The economy was beginning to suffer as a result of the prolonged mobilization.

Abba Eban reported to his colleagues on his talks in
Washington. The Americans thought they could do
something, but they wanted time, and the foreign minister thought it should be given to them. There were
angry arguments. How much time? Did they offer to defend Israel? Was Nasser in the desert for the health of
his troops or what?

With all of its divisions, this was still a Cabinet of
moderate men which hoped, if it did not unanimously
believe, that there were options between the terrible
poles of fight or surrender. By a vote of nine to nine the

Cabinet left the decision of what to do next to the Prime Minister. Mr. Eshkol said that Israel would give the Americans some time.

The next problem was the public demand for a new defense minister. Mr. Eshkol knew what this really meant: the people wanted Moshe Dayan, the conqueror of the Sinai. Yet that was not what the Prime Minister wanted; the situation was too delicate and the decision to give the Americans more time too difficult to maintain without having the mesmeric hero of 1956 funneling the pressures of the military establishment up to the highest political level.

As Levi Eshkol was struggling to keep the hawks out of his Cabinet, public opinion under control and the few remaining options open, King Hussein suddenly moved from his compartment on the historic landscape and performed the act which finally fused all the factions in Israel into the harsh and hopeless conclusion that there was, at last, no option between the poles of victory or surrender. Aqaba had already become insignificant and the Arab encirclement was developing as the paramount issue and key motivating force inside Israel. The nursery window had been shut when Nasser seized the Gulf of Aqaba. Hussein locked it and put sealer around the cracks by his gesture of May 30. On that day—Tuesday—he flew to Cairo and into the arms of his mortal enemy Nasser. To the Israelis the situation was right back at pre-war 1956 and Churchill's phrase had become a horrid Arab reality; the ring was closed.

Everything that Eshkol was trying to do in Israel finally came apart. The secretariat of Mapai rejected the Prime Minister's suggestion that General Dayan be made a vice premier and a sort of adviser while Yigal Allon became defense minister. The secretariat demanded that Eshkol turn the national defense over to

Dayan. Angrily, the Prime Minister turned to the key group in his coalition, the National Religious Party. Its leader, Moshe Shapiro, was adamant. He wanted Dayan as defense minister for quite a different reason; the National Religious Party was against war and thought that only a government which included General Dayan could beat off the public demands for a showdown with the Arabs. If General Dayan was not made defense minister, said Shapiro, the National Religious Party would leave the coalition. That would have meant the end of Levi Eshkol's government. He capitulated and a new government of national unity was created. It included Dayan as defense minister and two right-wingers, Joseph Shapiro and Manachem Begin. The hawks were in.

And the barometer kept falling.

On Thursday two brigades of the Iraqi army moved onto Jordanian territory and proceeded toward the West Bank, the most vulnerable part of Israel's 400-mile-long border with Jordan. Earlier on Thursday—at 2:30 a.m.—an Israeli patrol stumbled onto a band of armed Syrian terrorists who had been on a mine-planting expedition near Kfar Hanassi. After a brief, vicious gunfight, two Israelis lay dead and another was wounded. First blood had been drawn.

Avraham Harmon, the Israeli ambassador in Washington, was returning home for consultation. On Friday evening, June 2, he stopped by the State Department for a talk with Secretary Rusk. Harmon was accompanied by Ephraim Evron, the minister who had had the surprising encounter with President Johnson. Earlier that day Robert Anderson, the secret emissary, had come out of Egypt to Portugal and had filed a report of his talks with President Nasser. On the same afternoon the White House had received Nasser's reply to another Johnson appeal for calm. Both the Anderson report and the Nasser letter re-stated the Egyptian positions on the Gulf of Aqaba and the troop build-up in the Sinai. The adamance of the letter and of Nasser's talk with Anderson had caused deep gloom in the State Department. The only ray of hope—and it was a small one—was Nasser's agreement to send Zakariya Moheiddin to Washington for talks the next week. Harmon went on to the airport and Evron returned to Twenty-second Street to cable a report of the conversation to Jerusalem.

The depressing word from Washington was read by the Cabinet on Saturday, June 3. By then—with the encirclement the dominant fact of life, with Dayan, Shapiro and Begin in the Cabinet and the former moderates themselves now feeling pretty grim—everybody knew what was going to happen. Even the tiny hope held out by the Moheiddin visit to Washington turned into suspicion in Jerusalem. If a deal was struck that somehow conceded Nasser's right to hold on to Sharm El Sheik, the Israelis would have suffered their final loss—the sympathy for war that they regarded as imperative to their long-range interests.

Later on Saturday word came in from intelligence that a Syrian armored brigade was moving toward Jordan to assist in the attack from that front. Two Egyptian commando units had arrived at Sammua to prepare for the drive southwest that would cut the Negev in two.

It hardly mattered any more. The Egyptian and Syrian moves were more of the same, and the same was already too much.

General Dayan held his cheerfully deceptive press conference. The time for an immediate reaction to the seizure of Aqaba had passed and diplomacy must be given a chance. Had he and the rest of the Cabinet not known by then that war was inevitable, General Dayan would not have bothered to produce this artfully dragged red herring.

On Sunday the Cabinet met for most of the day. Everything was reviewed for a final time. Obviously, the Americans could be given no more time. Any diplomatic solution now—as the Cabinet saw it—would be written upon the tomb of Israel. Toward evening they voted to leave the final decision up to the Prime Minister and the defense minister. Every man in the room knew what the decision would be and when it would be acted upon. The risk of leaks was great, the upper globe of the glass timer was empty of sand and the moment had arrived when war was preferable to the prevailing situation.

And so, on Monday, it began.

The glorious part of war is relatively brief, the consequences fester on and on and the dead are dead forever. As long as one is neither participating in it nor watching it up close, the glorious part of war is a combination of palliative, diversion from the dullness of ordinary life and sports event. The thrilling hurtle of the juggernaut, the individual acts of bravery, the violence, danger and subsidiary dramas make men seem better than they are. The glorious part of war makes us forget the shortcomings of the winning side. It creates legends first and then the games of children.

When the glory passes and the consequences become a miasma of politics and economics, when the drone of statesmen and the wails of sorrow over the absent dead drown out the memory-echo of trumpets and guns, the world turns away from war and would just as soon not hear any more about it.

On Wednesday, June 7, the briefing officers arranged a trip into the Sinai for a group of correspondents in Tel Aviv. Rental cars fell in behind two buses commandeered from an agency that takes tourists around to see the various historic sights of Israel. It was another day of brilliant sun and a sky of flawless blue. In the desert the sun seemed larger and the whole sky was a nimbus of its white, static fire.

The party left Tel Aviv shortly after 9:00 a.m. and headed south on the main road to Beersheba, the principal city of the Negev. The briefing officers on the first bus said that the party would be taken into the Gaza Strip, out to the coastal Sinai fortress of El Arish and, by helicopter, southwest to Abu Agwila to see from the air the great tank battle which was still raging in the central desert. The bus radio played martial music which alternated with themes from Broadway shows and James Bond movies and news bulletins about the battlefronts. Intense fighting was raging in Jerusalem; the Israeli penetration into the Old City had begun and the Jewish quarter was under heavy shelling. The Jordanian radio station in Jerusalem had been captured. "That's too bad," one of the briefing officers said. "We won't hear the Arab classical hour this morning." In New York, the Soviets had withdrawn their demand for a return to the positions each side had occupied before the fighting began and had agreed to the United Nations Security Council call for a cease-fire at present locations. The Israeli correspondents on the bus greeted this news with ribald laughter.

The BBC said that six Arab states had broken relations with the United States. The American journalists on the bus looked out of the windows. The road led past an air base. Stumpy Mystères whirred in over the rolling landscape and dropped down onto the strips, keeping their wheels up until the last moment. The countryside was green, but it was not the thick, uniform green of rural Europe or North America; the grainfields of Israel are thinly planted. The soil is sandy and vegetation is interspersed with patches of bare, sun-baked earth. Nineteen years before, it had all been desert.

The road ran parallel to the mountains of Judea, which stood dull green in the heat haze off to the east. The convoy rolled past Waddi Faluga, where, in the war of 1948, Major Gamel Abdel Nasser of the royal Egyptian army had been besieged for weeks. (During the subsequent negotiations there, Major Nasser had questioned the Israelis closely about the techniques of Haganah and the other underground organizations that had struggled against the British in Palestine. He was about to embark upon a plotting struggle of his own against the flabby monarchy of Egypt.) The escorting briefing officers—one of them was an archaeologist in private life—pointed out a two-thousand-year-old track used by the Jews in their guerrilla wars against the Canaanites and mentioned that El Fatah terrorists had blown up a section of the Tel Aviv–Beersheba railroad line a few hours earlier. Like most Israelis, the briefing officers spoke of their own people's history as if it were as vividly alive as corpuscles and breath, and they discussed the Arabs with the clinical detachment one reserves for interesting but unaccomplished specimens of a somewhat removed order of life.

At 10:30 the buses pulled over to the side of the dusty road. Israeli troops were milling around—some dressed in tee shirts, khaki trousers and boots, others in sloppy uniforms two sizes too large or grown suddenly too small through the owner's acquisition of a pot belly; some men wore wide-brimmed Australian-style hats, some the comical little canvas fool's cap which is the trademark of light-hearted Israeli derring-do. All of them were dirty and hadn't shaved for several days. There were heavy-featured, unsmiling men with thick eyebrows and lips and strong noses and chins; some were

blond and blue-eyed, others had the scrawny, fleshless
look of Yemeni Jews; these latter people were brought
to Israel on the U.S. Air Force's Operation Magic Carpet
in 1948—the only occasion in history, perhaps, when a
Biblical prophecy was accomplished with military aircraft. All the men beside the road carried weapons of
some sort—hand grenades dangled from belts; pistols
were worn in loose canvas holsters that dangled western-
style low on the hip; there were gleaming, oiled machine
guns, and rifles and knives were thrust into boot tops.

The troops clustered around the buses as the correspondents climbed off. Greetings in Hebrew were
shouted back and forth, some of the soldiers called out
American and Canadian place names in English; the
troops ate as they talked, munching on chocolate bars
and drinking from tins of pineapple. One of the briefing
officers tried to find out who was in charge. Whoops
and shouts echoed back and forth and a man whose
pale epaulets and better-fitting uniform marked him as
an officer appeared over the rise of a low ridge in a field
beyond the road. He shook hands with the briefing
officers, shook his head, argued a few moments and
then nodded.

The place, it was explained, was called Mishmar
Hanegev—"Watch on the Negev"—and it was a sorting
area for prisoners brought in from the front. On the
other side of the ridge a stockade was being built; it
already contained some Egyptians and a few of the
Palestine Liberation Army irregulars from the Gaza
Strip.

The man in charge had been reluctant to let the correspondents see the prisoners because he hadn't the
proper authority to do it. The briefing officers said that
it was against the Geneva Convention regulations to let
anyone question or photograph prisoners; if the re-

porters would agree to abide by these rules, they could go over the ridge and have a look.

The stockade stood on a gentle slope tilting away from the ridge. At the far end—two hundred yards away—Egyptian prisoners were still uncoiling barbed wire and pounding tall stakes into the ground. At two corners of the big pen there were twelve-foot-high watchtowers. Israeli troops spaced ten feet apart sat on the ground with their caps over their foreheads to keep the sun off their eyes. Each man had a machine gun lying across his knees. They grinned at the correspondents.

Behind the wire fence the Egyptian prisoners also sat on the ground. They wore dust-gray uniforms and their caps had been taken away. Their common physical posture was the relaxed sag of depression; some sat cross-legged, heads bowed, fingers picking slowly at tufts of coarse grass; others sat with their legs bent and their arms resting on their knees, staring off into the hot grasslands. Some had bandaged heads or hands. As Israeli troops moved among them, the Egyptians raised their heads and—inaudible to the watching journalists—answered the questions being put to them in Arabic. The prisoners were war's classic waifs, and their faces, as they looked up at their captors, wore all the expressions of their condition. The men were mostly peasants from the Delta. Some looked up in fear, others in hatred; some were almost expressionless in the toneless antipathy of despair, and some had the forlorn, reproachful look of lost children.

Three men sat in an enclosure by themselves. They managed a gesture of dignity as movie cameras—despite warnings about the Geneva Convention—were pointed at them. The three men hitched around until their backs were to the correspondents and began to talk among themselves. The Israelis said that they were officers—a colonel and two majors. When this particular group surrendered near Rafah, the colonel had been heard to shout to his men, "Raise your hands and they'll treat you well."

The prisoners' personal possessions were being taken. The money, wristwatches and jewelry were put into paper bags and labeled. Several Egyptians were led off to a long shed outside the stockade for questioning. All of them would be moved farther to the rear later in the day for intensive interrogation. The most promising among them would, still later, be bathed, doctored and taken on tours of Israel before being sent home. In a Haifa supermarket a few weeks after the war an Egyptian officer recognized the manager as the man who had captured him in the Sinai. Though the concept of a citizen army may have been understood by the specially treated Egyptian prisoners along with other principles and habits of Israeli life, this campaign of sending truth-contaminated prisoners back to Egypt never paid off for the Israelis. After the 1956 war most of the returnees who had been given the treatment in Israel were either quarantined by the Egyptian authorities or told to keep their observations about the revealed Israel to themselves.

The convoy resumed its journey toward the Gaza Strip. As it approached the crossing point from Israel into former Egyptian territory, the clusters of troops and military equipment were more frequent. Soldiers stacked cartons of ammunition beside the road to be picked up by the supply convoys which moved into the desert at night; tanks and slender anti-aircraft guns were parked beneath gently swaying groves of willow trees. At one crossroads three Israelis drove up in a blue-and-white jeep captured from the United Nations camp in the Gaza Strip. ("Donated to our forces courtesy of

Nasser and U Thant," said one of the briefing officers.)

The convoy turned east and headed out across a desolate flatland of sand and hummocks tufted with brittle grass. "We are now crossing toward the Gaza Strip," the officer in the lead bus said. "Two days ago this was all minefields. And there was shelling from the other side. We took severe casualties here."

The road wound among the sand hummocks. The cars in the convoy soon bogged down and their occupants joined the buses. Twice the vehicles were stalled in low defiles of soft sand and everybody had to get out and push. The buses whirled their wheels, groaned, roared and finally lurched forward. At one place in the hot, desolate crossing Israeli soldiers were laying steel mats on the soft ruts. A spotter plane droned a few hundred feet overhead, circled and flew back to Israel. Columns of black smoke drifted up from the northwest. "A little activity still around the city of Gaza," one of the officers announced. "I assure you, you do not need to worry. Our troops can handle it." The radio was playing a loud medley of airs from *The Sound of Music*.

The abandoned watchtowers of the U.N. camp loomed ahead. At 12:33 the buses lurched up onto a tar road. "Welcome to the former Gaza Strip," an officer said, grinning. "You are now going into what was Israel, is again Israel and, I hope, will remain Israel." He was a small, blond man with a sharp-nosed face and a tiny mustache on his protruding upper lip.

The United Nations camp was deserted. Ten Indians had been killed there as the Israelis blasted their way through on Monday morning. The rest of the U.N. troops were said to be on a beach to the west, waiting for a Swedish ship to come and take them away. The camp they had left behind was a collection of wooden buildings, a basketball court and a cement parking lot where the U.N.'s captured blue-and-white vehicles had been neatly drawn up in a row. On the side of one building a huge sign read: DON'T SHOOT. WE ARE UNITED NATIONS TROOPS.

The buses rolled past a bleak, cactus-choked sand flat where bits of bramble, twigs and rubbish had been twisted together to make low, skeletal huts. The poorest of the Palestinian refugees had lived there as squatters. Each of the miserable little dwellings had a bit of white cloth attached to it, but the people were all gone; an expressionless donkey and a gaunt goat stood in the blazing sun. The donkey's eyes were closed. On the radio Julie Andrews was singing, "You are sixteen, going on seventeen. . . ."

Rafah is a railroad switchyard at the western end of the Gaza Strip. In 635 A.D. six thousand Jewish and Christian soldiers were slaughtered there by a Moslem army. In a simpler time of the twentieth century when colonialism and great-power politics kept all borders more or less permanently open, the Cairo-Istanbul-London express used to go through Rafah. On the early afternoon of June 7 a herd of sheep was wandering across the tracks; the houses and sheds of the village were riddled with bullet holes; a bent bicycle lay on the ground; and Israeli soldiers were swarming all over the place, waving rifles and shouting at the passing bus and walking around a group of shrouded Arab women who squatted in neat ranks on the ground. Some of them held their hands in front of them, palms together, as if in prayer. Their children played on the railroad tracks among the sheep.

The road west is the road into the Sinai.

It is a road that winds between sand dunes and patches of low scrub bush. Here and there a tree stands in martyrdom to the sun, and rude huts are uninhabitable ovens in the heat of the day. By tradition it is the road upon which the Holy Family fled west to escape the wrath of Herod, and the armies of Napoleon marched east along it on their way to Haifa. To senses developed in climates of water, green and wind, the Rafah–El Arish road is the ultimate wilderness. A desert is the arena of silence, and since nothing capable of noise lives in one, the hush of eternity hangs in the dry, scorched air; it is not as if life had departed but, rather, as if it had never been there.

The first visible dead Egyptian lay sprawled on the left side of the road among low shrubs. The corpse, when it was a man, had been running west, away from the Israelis bursting toward him from the east. It lay face down, arms stretched forward, legs bent, a black coat yanked up high around the shoulders. When the first dead soldier is seen, the battle which killed him shrivels inward in the mind of the observer; it ceases to be something of strategy, political motive and historic inevitability and becomes, in that dreadful moment, a matter of dry and immobile intimacy.

The road turned sharply south and sloped downhill. More bodies lay on either side, some face up, their flesh burned negroid black by the sun. Some wore no shoes— they had ripped them off in the timeless impulse of the running peasant. Others embraced the earth with their bent arms or had died with one forearm standing like a post, the hand open and the fingers spread as if to receive the gesture of oblivion with a certain grace. A bloated cow lay among the scattered human remains, and the only thing that lived upon the sand profaned by murder was a calf between the cow's spread and broken hind legs. It looked off into the blinding desert with a contemplative expression.

The first corpse shocks, sickens and, for a moment,

re-defines the war in terrible and intimate human terms. But as the sight of death proliferates, the meaning of war widens again and the dead become part of its index; if there are many of them, the art of battle has been executed with skill, and the observer feels a loathsome exultation rising in himself as he rides through the avenues of carnage. It is as if he possessed a special virtue by remaining alive while so many are lifeless around him. In this way he associates himself with the winners and then, suddenly, hates himself for forgetting that the dead were also once alive and deserve his tears.

The remains of an Egyptian tank rested on a slope off to the right. It was half ruined and half perfect; a shell had hit its underside, and the tank stood in a charred patch of its own burned fuel. The treads had been wrenched apart, bits of machinery lay about in the sand, but the upper half was still intact. The cannon pointed toward Rafah and the hatch was closed. Other vehicles in various states of destruction were scattered about on the sandy ridges: a troop carrier with one flat tire and the Egyptian eagle painted on its hood, a truck lying on one side, scorched tanks and an oblong mass of black tortured metal that could have been the remains of almost anything.

At a crossroads crowded with Israeli troops and gear and littered with Egyptian wreckage the buses turned west again. A violent fire-fight had taken place there two days before. Great treaded machines were hauling wrecked Egyptian equipment off the road; troops were climbing over tanks and half-tracks that had not been damaged at all. The unburned Egyptian vehicles were painted pale buff to match the color of the desert. The trucks bore the label of the state auto works at Gorky, U.S.S.R. Israeli troops had hung the boots of dead Egyptians on some; one truck had a photograph of

General Amer, the Egyptian chief of staff, wired onto its radiator. Israelis drove captured jeeps up and down the road, shouting and laughing like children who had taken over someone else's playroom. Some of them appeared to be little more than children—boys with curly hair, their shirts unbuttoned down to the waist, outsized canteens dangling from their belts. They whooped, laughed and made thumbs-up signs at the passing buses, and the rifles they waved seemed designed for larger men. Israeli equipment was mingled with the Egyptian junk along both sides of the road—two-wheeled water carriers, portable cooking units with chimneys, and mud-smeared vehicles drafted from civilian life: a farm truck, an ice-cream vender's van, a police car.

The buses drew to the side of the road to let a military convoy pass. A big truck with fence sidings squeezed by; it was full of Egyptian prisoners seated with their hands on their heads. They looked out from the shelter of their own arms at the laughing Israelis and the wreckage of their own army. Some saw the cameras in the press buses and their Arabic shouts of "Photograph! Photograph!" added to the general din of yelling Israelis and roaring engines. After the truckload of Egyptians there came a troop carrier with guards sitting on it, guns pointed at the prisoners. Some of them were stripped to the waist and wore silver Stars of David on chains about their necks. The convoy turned north and headed off toward Rafah past the black bodies of the Egyptian dead lying on the sand.

But if the sight of their colleague's corpses shocked the Egyptian prisoners, the impact must have diffused itself into sorrow and Arab fatalism by the time they passed the correspondents' buses; the road west of the junkyard was lined with bodies on either side—some flung away from the post-explosion wreckage of trucks, others maimed by machine-gun bullets, arms and legs broken, sides torn open; one corpse sat against a withered tree, its head bent to one side, lying upon the shoulder, raising the question of whether the man had crawled there to die or had been shot as he rested. The Egyptian dead were eventually put to earth by bulldozers of the Israeli army.

Here and there in the sun-blasted wilderness the Egyptians had made little camps around the concentration of their vehicles. Pits had been scraped out of the sides of sand dunes and trucks driven into them, some covered with camouflage netting. Higher up, tanks were dug into holes on the tops and sides of the dunes, their cannon still pointing east in a mockery of timing; the juggernaut had long since torn through on its way to El Arish, and the defending tanks stood like military buffoons who had come too late to fight but still posed themselves in ferocious postures of threat. Slender-barreled anti-aircraft guns stood on the high dunes packed around with sandbags. Through the wisps of shrubbery the stiff bodies of the gun crews could be seen, as empty of possibility as their equipment.

Fifteen kilometers east of El Arish the buses stopped near a deep declivity crisscrossed by cinder-block trenches, tents and rows of trucks, and circled on two sides by T-34 and Stalin-type tanks on the crests of the dunes. The flight of the Egyptians from that particular stronghold had been especially chaotic. Crates and cartons lay scattered about on the ground; through the open door of a shack, plates could be seen on a table with withered food left uneaten. Two trucks had been selectively blasted by rocket fire out of a row of six, and one tank was humped, blackened and crippled. Israeli troops dragged belts of ammunition toward the road and gunned tank engines. From the crest of a dune they danced and waved their foolish little caps.

The briefing officers said that the correspondents could get out but they were not, repeat, NOT to step off the road. Both verges were heavily mined; Israeli mop-up soldiers had already been killed by stepping on mines. The electronic sweepers had a lot of territory to cover and, besides, some of the mines were plastic and couldn't be located by the sounding devices.

The correspondents got out and one man promptly stepped off the road as he unzipped his fly. There was a loud shout, several reporters flung themselves onto the road surface while six pairs of hands bodily yanked the offender back. A stream of urine arched up into the sun. The reporter cursed and went behind a bus to finish relieving himself.

Souvenir bullets were picked up from the sand and the buses moved on. There were more bivouacs, more trenches and more bodies (the Rafah–El Arish road had already fallen prey to the journalist's penchant for naming everything that did not have a formal name of its own; the road had become "Corpse Alley" in five languages and two dozen notebooks). Every mile of the way produced more evidence of the Egyptians' panic and the violent power of the Israelis as they slammed through the enemy tanks, troops and cannon toward El Arish. There were no bodies in the trenches that snaked up and down the sand dunes, and none of the corpses arrested in the broken paralysis of death had weapons nearby. Most of them were shoeless, some clutched little copies of the Koran as a futile talisman. Foot tracks led up and over the sides of the dunes. In some places cannon fire or bombs had torn into groups of trucks, flinging them away from each other as the petrol tanks exploded.

The landscape grew flatter and wisps of smoke could

be seen off to the west and the south. Over the march-
ing racket of Kol Israel's triumphant music on the bus
radio the *mump!* of distant cannon sounded through the
open windows. To the right of the buses the railroad line
appeared out of the lower dunes. Boxcars lay on their
sides splintered apart or tossed up onto each other like
fornicating cattle.

Crowds of troops on vehicles or milling about in the
sunlight could be seen immediately ahead. A tall spire
topped by a stone eagle rose above them. A low ridge
decorated by gnarled trees stood to the north; through
its jagged gaps the even blue of the Mediterranean appeared with relieving symmetry. On to the west there
were a little yellow mosque, sheds and houses. Low
wooden buildings framed the crossroads where the
troops moved about. "This," said the briefing officer in
the first bus, "is as close as you get to El Arish. There
is still a little activity going on up ahead." Machine-gun
fire burst out in the sunlight, jabbering from a metal
throat. The sharp-faced officer leaned down and peered
through a window. "It appears that we have run into
some Egyptians who are willing to fight. The monu-
ment, by the way, is to commemorate their great victory in the Sinai in 1956. We'll stop here for ten minutes."

The Israeli army is one of the world's sloppiest to
look at and, in another way, one of the world's prettiest.
Its celebrated girl soldiers go close to the front, but don't
shoot unless they have to. They do signals and adminis-
trative work and act as medics. At the El Arish crossroads, girl soldiers sat on the flat beds of trucks, walked
about with clipboards checking things or stood looking
off to the west where black columns of smoke drifted up
from the bombarded town. The military girls of Israel
all seem to be good-looking; perhaps they appear so be-

cause of the dirty, messy men around them and the general carnage of the setting in which they work during wars. Unlike their male colleagues, the girl soldiers were all clean and neat—some had their hair tied up in bandannas. There were dark-eyed, black-haired girls of the Levant, snub-nosed Europeans with blond hair and a few who could have come in that morning from Regent Street, Fifth Avenue or the Champs-Elysées.

The disorder was so great at the El Arish crossroads that it seemed impossible that the Israelis were operating on any sort of plan at all. Truckloads of troops rumbled in from the south; men sat on the ground eating while others posed for pictures; vehicles cross-blocked each other in traffic snarls, drivers swore and shouted in Hebrew, men stood in the backs of cars and waved their arms while officers bawled orders that nobody paid any attention to. Egyptian prisoners in their underwear with hands clasped on the tops of their heads were trotted at double time through the chaos of vehicles and people while army girls watched. In the natural order of things, Arabs hold women to be inferior beings, and to be watched by a conquering lady while one is being prodded about in one's shorts must have produced a sense of humiliation that surpassed even hatred and fear.

The machine-gun fire started again beyond the ridge. Somebody whooped an order and a group of soldiers leaped into a jeep, which honked and twisted its way through the mess. It roared up the side of the ridge and disappeared over the top. The volume of machine-gun fire doubled for fifteen seconds. The jeep reappeared, skidding sideways down the dune; the troops grinned and one man waved a pistol in the air.

One-hundred-and-five-millimeter cannon were going off somewhere in the distance. Sniper fired opened up from the general direction of the little mosque. A mortar team wearing flat helmets covered with netting ran up, erected a tripod and barrel and dropped a mortar shell down the long steel throat. There was a sharp crack and the missile went whistling off into the sunlight.

The correspondents got back into their buses and the convoy started off into the south. "We are now taking you to the airport," the sharp-faced officer in the first bus said, "if we can manage to get ourselves out of here."

Two trucks that had been trying, simultaneously, to pass the bus on the left were wedged together hood to hood; a line of jeeps and troop carriers on the right of the bus was being mashed up against two tanks. A soldier standing in the back of one of the jeeps stuck his head and shoulders through the window of the bus and grasped a British correspondent's hand. "Hey, Mossman! You remember me? Six years ago I drive you all over Tel Aviv in the taxi!"

Someone yelled, "Mozzletof!"

The soldier, a black-haired man with a huge jaw and several teeth missing, roared with laughter. "Shalom!"

The bus inched forward, swamped by traffic and a welter of shouted directions and profanity. After the crossroads proper it eased into a street lined with trees and the remnants of houses. Everything made by man appeared to have been hit by mortar or artillery fire. Beneath a grove of little trees a group of women squatted looking at four rows of underwear-clad prisoners lying on the ground with their hands on their heads. Three Israelis with tommy guns wandered among them. The group of squatting women was ringed in with barbed wire.

All along the road to the airport there were patches

of trees, orchards and abandoned vegetable gardens. A spur rail line ran beside the road. An ammunition train had been parked opposite an army camp that was in among a cluster of trees. Rocket fire from the Mirage III's had hit the train on the first morning of the war. Half of the engine was intact; the other half had been melted into the long, blackened rubble of the train by the heat of the detonating ammunition. Smoke still curled up from the withered mass of steel and charred wood. Across the road in the army camp everything except the trees had been killed by the violent explosion of the train. Bloated corpses were scattered about, some with the trousers blown off of them so that the swollen genitalia were exposed. The body of an officer who had been standing in a tank turret was snapped at the waist; the upper half of the corpse, arms spread wide, lay on the hot metal deck of the tank while the legs still stood in the interior. The blackened face looked up into the sun with a macabre grin.

One-hundred-and-fives thundered in the afternoon; off on the horizon, columns of black smoke from El Arish drifted northeast. The oil tanks of the town had been hit and were burning.

The airport was the first one hit by the historic Israeli air strike on Monday morning. Out on its runways the mortally blasted bodies of MIG-21's and Sukhois lay in the sun. The buses pulled up in front of an administration building shaded by trees. Israeli troops were throwing sand on one of their portable cookers that had caught fire. Helicopters clattered overhead, going west into the Sinai battlefield, going east to Israel. Across the cement expanse of the field, runways were being cleared and prisoners were being herded down into a pit. The Israeli base commander, Colonel Yerocham Amitai, came out and talked to the briefing officers. He was a stocky, pleasant-faced man in an impeccable summer uniform. A German concentration-camp number was tattooed on his wrist.

The sharp-faced briefing officer climbed back into the first bus. "Bad news," he said. "Bad for you and bad for us. We are taking a lot of casualties this afternoon around here and the helicopters are needed to carry them to the rear. There will be no flights over the battle-field."

For an hour the correspondents wandered around the airfield, awed by the strange sense of absenteeism that is always inherent in captured territory, looking at the destroyed artifacts of the departed—a metal hangar with the burned skeleton of an Ilyushin-14 transport beneath a roof riddled with more than a hundred jagged holes; the smashed remnants of fighters on the strips; a little club building for the Egyptian officers, its refrigerator door hanging open, papers and magazines scattered about the floor. One reporter picked up a page from an American Bible tract. A little corn patch behind the club building rustled in the warm wind.

An Israeli troop carrier drove across the concrete landing strip. Inside, two wounded men lay groaning on the metal floor. One was a muscular boy in his early twenties with blond hair. He held his blood-caked hands over his stomach and whimpered while an army girl bathed his head with a wet rag. All of the warrior had been torn from him at the moment when he had been shot; his uniform, his muscular forearms and his heavy boots were that part of him which remained a man. But the face that looked up at the medics who came to lift him out was that of a child stricken with a vision of the incomprehensible. He jerked and sank his teeth into his arm as they put him on a stretcher. A terrible, bellowing cry burst from behind his gnawing teeth. The girl turned toward the other man as the boy was eased out and carried toward a helicopter.

The second man was either unconscious or in shock. His right leg had been nearly torn off by shell fragments. He, too, was lifted out and carried to the helicopter. By the time he had arrived the body of the boy was being taken back out of the aircraft. A jacket had been put over his face. The arm with teeth marks still on it hung limply over the side of the stretcher.

The correspondents got back into the buses. Helicopters clattered overhead and the cannon thumped in the distance. On the way back to the crossroads the buses passed a group of Israelis playing soccer; a little distance away another man squatted with his trousers down and a rifle across his knees.

At four o'clock the radio music abruptly stopped and an excited announcer said, in Hebrew, that Israeli naval forces had captured Sharm El Sheik, beating out a company of paratroopers who had been on their way to the same objective. The correspondents on the buses cheered. The offense that had provoked the war had been rectified without the firing of a shot. But the Gulf of Aqaba had become irrelevant; once wars start, they develop a new logic and a new perspective. It is no longer sufficient to eradicate the original aggression. The winning side resurrects older grievances and wider plans and these become the new reasons for the war. This one still had three days to run and its new logic remained to be accomplished.

At 4:35 the announcer broke into the music again and said that the Old City of Jerusalem had fallen. Again the bus resounded with cheers, and the sardonic, sharp-faced officer had tears in his eyes. "I can tell you," he shouted, "this is the greatest day of my life! Jerusalem! Now, there's something I can tell you about!"

In the dusk the correspondents wandered back across the Sinai, across the desolate wilderness where life had not been intended, where life had come anyway and had been destroyed. The Israelis who had been scattered all down the length of Corpse Alley had got themselves reorganized and columns were moving into the desert; the sun hung in a red dust blaze in the west, and the sudden cool of the Sinai's night came out of the darkness that approached across the world from the east. At one place an Israeli tank had hit a mine; its turret had been ripped off as by a blunt can-opener and its fiery remnants were scattered across the road.

The stars were out as the buses rolled through Rafah. Convoys were coming across the no-man's-land on the far side of the deserted United Nations camp. The buses drew to the side of the road as trucks groaned up from the sandy waddis and lumbered off toward El Arish. Wrecked Egyptian tanks and trucks were hauled back in the opposite direction with frightful roarings of engines and meshing of gears. The darkness of the crossing was strung with headlights in a jeweled stream reaching back to Israel. Jerusalem Radio came on with a live broadcast from the Wailing Wall. General Rabin's deep voice boomed through the speakers; the microphones picked up babbles, shouts and the flat wail of the shofar being blown in the exultant excitement of a people returned. In the darkness at the crossing a six-foot-seven-inch officer with black crisp hair and a huge face sat down in the dust, raised his eyes to the stars and wept. Jerusalem had not been forgotten and the right hand of the Jews had not lost its terrible cunning.

At last the buses returned across another road. Artillery whumped off to the west in the Gaza Strip and mortar shells arched in the cold gloom. Again the buses floundered in the soft sand and everyone got out and pushed. The stars were close to the earth and a soft halo of fire broached the northern horizon.

Upon the main Israeli highways long lines of trucks waited to make the crossing. They stood bumper to bumper; in the glow of the headlights the drivers' faces were tired. Thursday morning had come in darkness, cold and the victorious peal of the ram's horn. The buses rolled back toward Tel Aviv, past the convoys waiting to go into the desert where the Jews fought on in the new logic of their war.

Jordan had quit on Wednesday. The King who had triggered but not, necessarily, caused the war—the one Arab leader who could have kept his country immune from it—was the first to leave the battlefield. For Hussein it had been an adventure in ignominy; he had been panicked into fighting and he had lost everything that counted except his personal dignity. At midnight the government of Israel made an announcement which confirmed that wars create new logics and put old plans into motion; the Israeli defense forces "having attained their objectives in reaching the Hills of Hebron and the Jordan River," Israel had decided to agree that Jordan was out of the fight.

Egypt stayed in for one more day, and, in a very real sense, it was her best day while, at the same time, it was her worst—the day of her defeat. On that Thursday the Egyptian remnants in the Sinai clawed and battered their way west, engaging the Israelis in tank battles that were fought in reverse but with a valor that, while it arose from desperation, stirred some of the Israeli commanders to admiration. Egyptian jets flew what amounted to suicide missions over the desert; as fast as they roared east out of the Delta to help the fleeing ground forces, they were smashed out of the sky by Mirage III's and

Mystères. The Mitla Pass had turned into a slaughter-house for Egyptian armor. Israeli forces commanded the hills that run down the west side of the Sinai twenty miles from the Suez Canal. Egyptian reserve forces came pouring across the canal at Ismailia, Qantara and Suez to fight. At one point during the day several Egyptian tank companies at Bir Gifgafa turned and hurtled themselves back onto the Israelis; they were battered and destroyed. The Israeli armored columns were rushing west so fast that some of the tanks ran out of fuel. Chains were thrown on them and they were hauled to the east end of the Mitla Pass, where they were used as artillery to blast the Egyptians fighting toward home.

By evening the government in Cairo had accepted the cease-fire.

Wars do not end when the last shot is fired, the last objective is taken or the surrender is signed. War is the interplay of mass and movement raised to the ultimate level of scientific savagery. When the greater part of the mass is destroyed on one side and when the maximum capacity to move has passed, when it becomes impossible for the defeated side to employ its remaining mass in movement equivalent to that of the winning side, the war is over. Fighting goes on, men die, the fortunes of this company or that brigade may waver—but this activity no longer has the potential of changing the outcome. War will never be a civilized process, but it will be less tragic when this definition of its end is accepted by armies in the field and they stop fighting at that moment when the outcome is no longer in doubt.

For the Israelis on Thursday night the Syrians still had to be dealt with. Some of the bravest and cruelest fighting remained. But the Syrians themselves had no hope of changing the final result and they didn't have much stomach for the sort of war they had to fight. They had thought for several years that taking on the Israelis with conventional weapons and tactics on a conventional battlefield was stupid, old-fashioned and ideologically incorrect. Their own subsequent defeat and the destruction of the hated Jordanians and the distrusted Egyptians were a paradoxical victory for Syria; in the shambles and ashes she could taunt her fellow losers with the claim that the doctrine of Damascus had been right all along. The way to get at the Israelis, according to the doctrine, was through a Popular War of sabotage, terrorism and guerrilla tactics. It didn't matter how long the process took. There was a paradox upon the paradox; if the Syrians could claim they were right at the end, they were totally wrong in the beginning. It was their Popular War which had started the whole wretched mess in the first place.

And so the third Arab-Israeli war was over, though the fighting went on and the extent of the consequences could not, at that stage, be fully imagined. The minister of information, Israel Galili, already had forebodings. "There is no doubt," he said, "that various political factors may exert pressure on Israel with a view to depriving her of essential gains made for her security."

On Friday, June 9, there was no more joy in Tel Aviv. The Jews are not a people who relax in victory. There never was a celebration of the war's extraordinary outcome in Israel. The short-term bravery and confidence of the Israelis at war give way to the old Diasporic anxieties; the implications of what had happened were beginning to be seen. At a terrible cost in life and fortune Israel had restored the status quo in a slightly better form. The choice of action had been forced upon her by uncontrollable events, but the bargain was not especially good. No matter what anyone in the outside world said, the Israelis as a whole would have preferred that the war had never happened.

In victory Israel suffers peculiar persecutions at the hands of her friends. Not only do governments try to dictate the terms that Israel shall dictate, but, also, the journalism and literature of Europe and North America work up a portrait of the Israelis as strutting conquerors enjoying their conquest. Obscene casualty comparisons are made which end with the conclusion that the Israelis have finished ahead of the game because their dead were slightly below 700 in number against thousands killed on the other side. As well as being morbid vulgarity, this is statistical nonsense. Given the Israeli population, that number of dead is equivalent to an American loss of 70,000. In victory Israel assumed, for the third time, the burden of an unbearable legend; her people had become the invincible Arab-killers of the East with all the arrogance and bestiality of character that the legend implies. Such a fiction may be useful to the legend-hungry, but it denigrates the complex civilization of Israel and it dehumanizes her people.

On Friday the Israelis buried their dead. In an airline office four girls listened to an American correspondent's recollections of the trip through the Sinai. In a foolish attempt to please, he told about the dirty, victorious armies, the mop-up at El Arish and the might of Israel as symbolized by the death and wreckage down Corpse Alley. When he had finished, one of the girls had tears in her eyes, and for a moment the American thought he had surpassed himself in stirring narrative. "How terrible," the girl said. "Oh, how terrible it must have been."

That evening after dark a taxi came to the blacked-out Tel Aviv Hilton to take the correspondent to the airport. The driver was a Yemeni, a cheerful and garrulous man who spoke about four hundred words of English— constantly. He had served with the British in World

War II, he said. He liked being a soldier, especially a British soldier even though the language had caused him some trouble at first. "They tell me to go march this and I march something else. Then they tell me I am so stupid and they don't know what they must do with me."

All the same, he had had a fine time in the Jewish Brigade. At first the American was interested in the conversation. "Listen, Mister," the Yemeni said, "pardon me, but I am going to tell you something. My parents come here sixty years ago. I am born here."

"You're a sabra, then."

The Yemeni grinned and his dark, yellow-toothed grin was seen in the dim lights of the dashboard. "That's me. Sabra. Listen, pardon me, but I am going to tell you something. All my life I live with the Arabs. I know Arabs. Arabs live upstairs—same food, same money, same job as me. Everything is fine. I go out and Arabs go out. I talk to them. They talk to me. Everything fine. What for do I want to go in Damascus?"

"No reason, I'm sure," the American said.

"I already been in Damascus. Cairo. Beirut. All those places. Cairo is very nice. But what for do I want to go in Cairo or Damascus?"

"No reason, I'm sure," the American said.

"I got in Israel my house, my wife, my job. I don't need to go in Cairo or Damascus."

"I'm sure," the American said. "Were you in the war here?"

The Yemeni grinned again. "Army in the day, drive taxi in the night. In the day they tell me to go that place and I take my gun and go."

"Where have you been in the last few days?"

The Yemeni laughed. "I make that my secret. If I tell you, maybe you tell Nasser. Listen, I am going to tell you something. All the Arabs go out of Israel. We pay for that land with money. All the Arabs go out. . . ."

"Some stayed."

". . . all the Arabs leave Israel. Now they stay in Damascus and I stay in Israel. Okay? What's the matter with that? If I don't want to go in his place, why he want to come in my place?"

"No reason, I'm sure," the American said.

Tel Aviv was gone in the eastern darkness. The artillery was sputtering out in the cold Sinai. Jordan mourned her lost land, her dead children and her own folly. Ragged and forlorn, armies of refugees were moving across the Middle East again to compound the despair that had symbolized the Arabs' reasons for war. The forces of Israel faced north, and last blood still had to be spent. Between Tel Aviv and Lydda the night was soft and warm. When the taxi's headlights flashed on momentarily, the rows of vegetables and the slender shapes of trees were seen briefly in the gloom. The land looked the same at the end as it had in the beginning. Victory is only an undisturbed Israel minus the men who had to die to keep it that way.

"So," the Yemeni was saying, "if I don't want to go in his place, he must not want to come in my place. Right?"

"Right," said the American.

Give me the grace to think as a man about what I have seen. War, according to Clausewitz, is the prerogative of the defender. It starts only when the defender refuses to surrender his vital interests. Yet what king can ever unravel so black a matter and how can such a thing be charitably disposed of when blood is its argument? *Redeem me from exultation at the sight of death.*

"I got nothing for Arab and he got nothing for me. So what he want to fight for? I got my job, my house fair and square. Right?"

"Right," said the American.

Off in the darkness to the right, jet engines keened on a ramp. They were not the engines of Mirage III's or Mystères but 707's, promising the normalcy of flights to everywhere with hot meals included. The skies were wiped and the airlines could cross them again. Victory for Israel was only a little more than there had been before; but defeat for the Arabs meant that there would be much less than there used to be. The illusion had been broken, the gap between the two realities had been rudely closed by a bridge of evident fire. The dream of Aiyamu-Arab would be painful in the resurrection. Humiliation would shriek for a new restoration of pride in the stunned silence of the soul, and the imagining of the next victory would have to be even more hateful than this one had been in order to accommodate the new shame.

"I think I talk too much," the Yemeni said.

Only the check-out counters were lit at Lydda airport. In the dim, crowded departure hall an old man with a long white beard, watery eyes and clothes of rabbinical black squirmed and shoved his way among people and baggage to get to the head of the exit line. It was as if his whole life had been spent in planning or making emergency departures from threatening places. In such an old life, anxiety is born of memory, not instinct.

Flights were announced for Athens, Rome and Paris.

Children cried and an American woman made a scene at the immigration desk.

The flight to London was announced. There were only nine passengers. As an attendant held a flashlight, they were squeezed one by one through a partially opened glass door and pointed toward a huge jet that squatted on the tarmac in the dark.

A policeman checked each boarding pass under the

rays of the flashlight. As the passengers walked toward the aircraft, the attendant said to each, "Shalom." In Israel the word is used for hello and good-bye.

But it really means peace.

In the land. In the soul.

Roderick MacLeish

Roderick MacLeish is a television and radio commentator for the Westinghouse Broadcasting Company. He worked abroad for many years as a correspondent, traveling through eastern and western Europe, the Middle East and the Far East. Author of one novel and innumerable newspaper and magazine articles, he has also written film documentaries in Britain and the United States. Mr. MacLeish is presently based in Washington.